Recipes for Comfort

Gooseberry Patch

A Country Store In Your Mailbox®

A Country Store In Your Mailbox®

Gooseberry Patch
600 London Road
Department Book
Delaware, OH 43015
★

1-800·854·6673

Copyright 2000, Gooseberry Patch 1-888052-80-5
Second Printing, October, 2001

How To Subscribe

Would you like to receive
"A Country Store in Your Mailbox"®?
For a 2-year subscription to our 96-page
Gooseberry Patch catalog, simply send $3.00 to:

Gooseberry Patch
600 London Road
Department Book
Delaware, OH 43015

Contents

Dedication

For all who celebrate the simple pleasures each & every day.

warm thoughts & wishes

Appreciation

Warmest "THANKS" to those who shared their most comforting & delicious recipes with us!

Gooseberry Patch
149 Johnson Drive
Delaware, Ohio

yum.

Savory Morning Fare

Hearty breakfasts of bacon & eggs, toast slathered with real butter, Hot coffee & Belgian waffles to be savored over a leisurely morning.

the good life

Ham & Apple Filled Puffed Pancake

Gail Prather
Bethel, MN

A hearty way to start your day!

3 T. butter, divided
3/4 c. milk
2/3 c. all-purpose flour
2 eggs

1/2 t. salt
1 c. cooked ham, cubed
21-oz. can apple pie filling
1 c. Cheddar cheese, shredded

In a 9" glass pie plate, melt 2 tablespoons butter in oven. In a large bowl, combine milk, flour, eggs and salt. Using a wire whisk, beat until smooth; pour batter into pie plate. Bake, uncovered, at 400 degrees for 20 to 25 minutes or until golden brown. Meanwhile, in a 10" skillet, melt remaining butter until sizzling; add ham and apple pie filling. Cook over medium heat, stirring occasionally, until heated through. Spoon filling into center of hot pancake; sprinkle with cheese. Cut into wedges. Makes 4 servings.

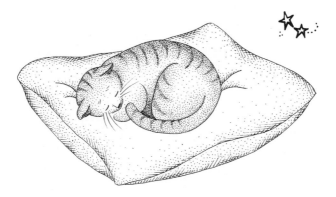

Comfort is...
Dozing in a warm, cozy spot with your cat.

Southern Pecan French Toast

Lori Roget
Post Falls, ID

One of those great recipes that you start the night before and just pop in the oven in the morning.

1 loaf French bread, sliced
6 eggs
1/4 t. nutmeg
1/2 t. cinnamon
1 t. vanilla extract
1-1/2 c. milk

1-1/2 c. half-and-half
1/2 c. butter, softened
1 c. brown sugar, packed
3 T. corn syrup
1 c. chopped pecans

Place as many bread slices as will fit in a single layer in a 13"x9" pan coated with non-stick vegetable spray. In a mixing bowl, combine eggs, nutmeg, cinnamon, vanilla, milk and half-and-half; pour over the bread slices. Cover and refrigerate overnight. In the morning, blend together butter, brown sugar, corn syrup and pecans. Spread over the bread slices. Bake, uncovered, at 350 degrees for 40 minutes or until golden brown. Makes 6 to 8 servings.

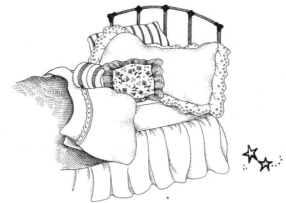

Comfort is...
Waking up to birds singing, sunshine and a clear, blue sky.

Cheddar & Bacon Breakfast Sandwiches   *Vickie*

Try Monterey Jack or Swiss cheese for a variety of flavor!

3 eggs, beaten
1/4 c. milk
2 T. butter
8 thick slices bread

12 slices Cheddar cheese
1/2 T. chopped walnuts
4 slices bacon, crisply cooked
   and crumbled

In a large bowl, whisk together eggs and milk; set aside. Prepare a griddle or large skillet by melting butter over low heat. Dip only one side of 4 bread slices in egg mixture. Place 4 bread slices, coated side down, on griddle or in skillet. Top each bread slice with 3 cheese slices. Sprinkle cheese with an equal amount of walnuts and bacon. Dip only one side of the remaining 4 bread slices in egg mixture and place over walnuts and bacon, coated side up. Cook 5 minutes per side or until bread is golden and cheese is melted. Makes 4 sandwiches.

Comfort is...
gardening on a cool day.

Fluffy Baked Eggs

Amy Butcher
Columbus, GA

Add a new twist to breakfast with sweet pineapple!

14 eggs, beaten
1 lb. sliced bacon, crisply cooked
    and crumbled, 2 T. drippings
    reserved
1-1/3 c. cottage cheese

8-oz. can crushed pineapple,
    drained
1 t. vanilla extract
Garnish: fresh parsley, chopped

Blend together eggs, bacon, drippings, cottage cheese, pineapple and vanilla; spoon into a greased 11"x7" baking dish. Bake, uncovered, at 350 degrees for 40 to 45 minutes or until center is set and tests done. Allow baking dish to set 5 minutes before slicing. Garnish with parsley, then cut into squares. Makes 8 servings.

Comfort is...
Finding the pair of earrings you
wanted on sale for half price.

Strawberry Surprise Scones

Marla Arbet
Burlington, WI

These are wonderful, light scones with strawberry jam inside! My family enjoys these and my kids get a kick out of eating them.

1 c. all-purpose flour
1 c. whole-wheat flour
3 T. sugar, divided
1 T. baking powder

1/4 c. butter, sliced
2/3 c. milk
1 egg, beaten
1/3 c. strawberry jam

In a large bowl, combine flours, 2 tablespoons sugar and baking powder. Cut in butter until mixture resembles coarse crumbs. Stir in milk and egg until just combined. Transfer dough to lightly floured surface and knead about 4 times until dough just holds together. Divide dough in half. Roll one half into an 8-inch circle and place on a greased baking sheet. Spread jam on top, leaving a one inch border. Roll remaining dough into an 8-inch circle and place on top. Press edges lightly to seal; sprinkle with remaining sugar. Cut into 8 wedges, but do not separate. Bake at 425 degrees for 20 minutes. Makes 8 scones.

Comfort is...
a peanut butter and jelly sandwich with fresh strawberry jam.

Sweet Fruit & Cream

Zoe Bennett
Columbia, SC

Yummy and healthy...what more could you ask for!

4 oz. cream cheese, softened
2 c. plain yogurt
3/4 c. quick-cooking oats,
   uncooked
3/4 c. chopped pecans
1/2 c. strawberries, sliced
1/2 c. grapes, halved

1/2 c. flaked coconut
1 banana, sliced
1 apple, chopped
2 t. lemon juice
3/4 c. whipping cream
sugar to taste

In a mixing bowl, blend together cream cheese and yogurt. Using an electric mixer, beat at medium speed for 2 minutes or until well blended. Stir in the oats, pecans, strawberries, grapes, coconut, banana, apple and lemon juice; set aside. In a large chilled mixing bowl, combine whipping cream with sugar. Beat at medium-high speed until soft peaks form; fold in fruit mixture. Makes 8 servings.

Comfort is...
   A dollop of whipped cream on your pancakes.

A wonderful way to begin your day

Coconut Coffee

Robin Hill
Rochester, NY

The coconut adds a taste of the islands to this coffee.

2 c. milk
3-1/2 oz. can flaked coconut
2 c. hot coffee
1/4 c. rum extract

Garnish: whipped topping,
coconut, toasted and finely
chopped almonds, toasted

Combine milk and coconut in a saucepan. Heat over medium-low until mixture steams; stir occasionally. Pour hot mixture into an electric blender, cover and blend on high speed until smooth. Using the same saucepan, blend together milk and coffee; heat well, but do not bring to a boil. Remove saucepan from heat; stir in the rum extract and divide among 4 coffee cups. Top each serving with a dollop of whipped topping, coconut and almonds. Makes 4 servings.

Mocha-Almond Coffee Mix

Rachel Burns
Elko, NV

Spoon into a sponge-painted jar tied with homespun and a handmade gift tag.

26-oz. can hot cocoa mix
1 c. plus 2 T. instant
   decaffeinated coffee granules

1-1/2 t. vanilla extract
1 t. almond extract

Mix all ingredients in a medium bowl. Store in an airtight container. To serve, add 3 heaping teaspoons of mix to one cup hot water and mix. Makes approximately 50 to 60 servings.

Comfort is...
Laughing out loud for no reason at all.

Buttermilk Pancakes

Jackie Crough
Salina, KS

These pancakes are good and so easy to make...have the kids help!

1 c. all-purpose flour	3 T. sugar
1 t. baking powder	1 egg
1/2 t. baking soda	2 T. butter, melted
1/2 t. salt	1 c. buttermilk

In a large mixing bowl, blend all ingredients together. Place one tablespoon of batter onto lightly greased skillet. Cook until bubbling, flip and cook other side. Makes 16 to 18 mini pancakes.

Comfort is...
squishing your feet in the sand on a beach.

A wonderful way to begin your day

Sour Cream Waffles

Deanna Brasch
Waterloo, IA

Delightful for a casual family brunch.

1 c. all-purpose flour
1 t. baking soda
1 t. baking powder
1 t. salt

2 eggs, separated and divided
1 c. sour cream
2/3 to 3/4 c. milk

Mix together dry ingredients. Add egg yolks and sour cream. Pour in milk until batter is of a pancake consistency. In a separate bowl, beat egg whites until stiff; fold into flour mixture. Cook in greased waffle iron until lightly brown. Makes approximately 5 waffles.

Comfort is...
A cool pillow on a hot summer night.

Baked Texas Orange French Toast

Sherry Rogers
Stillwater, OK

Serve with scrambled eggs and sausage for a big, country breakfast!

1/2 c. butter, melted
1/4 c. honey
2-1/2 t. cinnamon, divided
6 eggs
1/4 c. sugar
1 c. half-and-half
1 c. orange juice

2 t. orange zest
16 slices Texas toast
6-oz. can frozen orange juice
   concentrate, thawed and
   heated
Garnish: powdered sugar and
   orange slices

In a small bowl, combine butter, honey and 2 teaspoons cinnamon. Divide mixture evenly into 2 ungreased 15"x10" jelly roll pans. In a separate bowl, beat eggs and add sugar, half-and-half, orange juice, orange zest and remaining cinnamon; mix well. Dip toast slices into egg mixture and place in prepared pans in single layers. Pour any remaining egg mixture over bread. Bake at 400 degrees for 10 minutes, turn slices over and bake an additional 10 minutes or until golden brown. Slice diagonally and place 3 to 4 halves on serving plate. Drizzle with warm orange juice concentrate, garnish with powdered sugar and orange slices. Makes 8 to 10 servings.

Comfort is...
napping on a rainy afternoon.

A wonderful way to begin your day

Honeyed Fruit & Rice

Marilyn Epley
Stillwater, OK

Jasmine rice is commonly known as fragrant rice and can be found in many markets or specialty stores.

2 c. jasmine rice, cooked
1/3 c. dried cranberries
1/3 c. dried apricots, chopped

1/4 c. honey
milk

Mix together rice, dried cranberries, apricots and honey. Pour milk over rice to taste. Makes 2 servings.

Spinach-Cheddar Quiche

Mary Rita Schlagel
Warwick, NY

Try using any of your favorite green, leafy vegetables for a unique taste!

2 c. Cheddar cheese, shredded
2 T. all-purpose flour
10-oz. pkg. frozen, chopped
    spinach, cooked
1 c. milk
2 eggs, beaten

3 slices bacon, crisply cooked
    and crumbled
salt and pepper to taste
9-inch pastry shell, baked
Garnish: paprika and fresh
    parsley, chopped

In a large bowl, combine the cheese and flour; add spinach, milk, eggs, bacon, salt and pepper. Blend well and pour into pastry shell. Bake at 350 degrees for one hour. Garnish with paprika and parsley. Makes 4 servings.

Comfort is...
Sledding after a fresh snowfall.

Brown Sugar Sticky Buns

*Julie Clark
Lewiston, ID*

Enjoy a big glass of milk with these!

18 frozen dough balls
5-1/4 pkg. instant vanilla
   pudding mix

1/2 c. brown sugar, packed
1 t. cinnamon
1 stick butter

Place dough balls in an ungreased 13"x9" pan. In a medium mixing bowl, combine pudding mix, brown sugar and cinnamon; sprinkle over dough balls. Melt butter and pour over dough balls. Let sit uncovered in oven, overnight. Bake at 325 degrees for approximately 20 minutes; watch carefully. When done, immediately pour into a large bowl, making sure buns are covered with brown sugar mixture. Remove from bowl and place on a serving plate. Makes 18 buns.

Comfort is...
*Hearing a song that reminds you
of someone you love.*

Sunshine Grits

Regina Vining
Warwick, RI

A down-home, delicious comfort food.

3 c. water
1 t. salt
1 c. quick-cooking grits,
    uncooked
1 c. orange juice

1/4 c. butter
4 eggs, beaten
1-1/2 t. orange zest
2-1/4 T. brown sugar, packed

Bring water and salt to a boil in a 3-quart saucepan. Pour in grits and cook over medium heat for 3 minutes, stirring constantly; remove from heat. Stir in orange juice, butter, eggs and orange zest. Spoon into a greased 1-1/2 quart baking dish; sprinkle with brown sugar. Bake at 350 degrees for 45 minutes or until a knife inserted in the center comes out clean. Makes 8 servings.

Comfort is...
Watching a beautiful sunset.

Blueberry 'n Cheese Coffee Cake

Linda Hendrix
Moundville, MO

The perfect breakfast for your family's sweet tooth.

1/2 c. plus 2 T. butter, softened
    and divided
1-3/4 c. sugar, divided
2 eggs
2-1/2 c. all-purpose flour,
    divided
1 t. baking powder

1 t. salt
3/4 c. milk
1/4 c. water
2 c. blueberries
8-oz. pkg. cream cheese, cubed
    and softened
2 T. lemon zest

In a mixing bowl, beat 1/2 cup butter at medium speed until creamy; gradually adding 1-1/4 cup sugar and beat well. Add eggs one at a time, beating well after each addition. In a small mixing bowl, combine 2 cups flour, baking powder and salt; stir well. In a separate bowl, combine milk and water; stir well. Add flour mixture to butter mixture alternately with milk mixture. Mix at low speed after each addition until mixture is well blended. Gently stir in blueberries and cream cheese. Pour batter into a greased 11"x7" pan. In a medium bowl, combine remaining flour, sugar, lemon zest and butter; sprinkle mixture over batter. Bake, uncovered, at 375 degrees for 50 to 55 minutes or until golden. Serve warm. Makes 12 to 16 servings.

Comfort is...
    Hugging your mom and dad.

A Wonderful way to begin your day

Scrambled Egg Casserole

Diane Sybert
Athens, IL

A hit every time!

1/2 c. butter, divided
2 T. all-purpose flour
1/2 t. salt
1/8 t. pepper
2 c. milk
1 c. American cheese, shredded
1 c. cooked ham, cubed

1/4 c. green onions, sliced
12 eggs, beaten
4-oz. can sliced mushrooms, drained
1-1/2 c. soft bread crumbs, divided

In a medium saucepan, melt 2 tablespoons butter. Add flour, salt and pepper. Cook and stir until mixture begins to bubble. Gradually stir in milk; cook until thick and bubbly, stirring constantly. Remove from heat. Add cheese, mix well and set aside. In a large skillet, sauté ham and onions in 3 tablespoons butter until onions are tender. Add eggs, cook and stir until they begin to set. Add mushrooms and cheese mixture; blend well. Pour into a greased 11"x7" baking dish. Melt remaining butter; toss with one cup of bread crumbs. Sprinkle remaining bread crumbs over top of casserole. Cover and refrigerate for at least 2 to 3 hours or overnight. Bake, uncovered, at 350 degrees for 25 to 30 minutes. Makes 6 to 8 servings.

Comfort is...
The smell of freshly-brewed coffee.

Sausage-Biscuit Balls

Kelly McDermott-Bay
Chesterfield, MO

Perfect for a quick and easy breakfast.

1 lb. hot ground sausage
2 c. Cheddar cheese, shredded

2-1/2 c. biscuit baking mix

Mix all ingredients together, roll into balls. Place on ungreased baking sheet. Bake at 350 degrees for 15 to 20 minutes. Makes 10 to 12 servings.

Orange Toast

Arlene Boedecker
Hickory Hills, IL

Yummy topped with cream cheese!

1/4 lb. butter
1 c. sugar

2 T. orange zest
2 loaves bread, thinly sliced

Mix together butter, sugar and orange zest. Spread generously onto one side of each bread slice. Cut bread slices into 3 strips. Place bread on ungreased baking sheets. Bake at 250 degrees for 45 minutes to one hour. Be sure to check bread often as it hardens very quickly. Remove from baking sheet and let cool. Makes 20 servings.

Comfort is...
Breakfast in bed.

Cabin Dollar Pancakes

Diane Wolfe
Chico, CA

Just right for a breakfast buffet!

2 to 3 T. all-purpose flour
2 eggs, beaten
2 t. sugar

1/2 t. baking soda
1/8 t. salt
1 c. sour cream

In a large mixing bowl, mix together flour, eggs, sugar, baking soda, salt and sour cream. Batter will be thin. Drop batter by tablespoonfuls into a lightly greased skillet. Makes 15 to 20 dollar-sized pancakes.

Merry Berry Syrup

Jill Valentine
Jackson, TN

Drizzle your pancakes or waffles with this tasty syrup!

1-2/3 c. water
2/3 c. sugar
2 T. corn syrup
2 T. cornstarch
3-oz. pkg. raspberry gelatin mix

8-oz. pkg. frozen raspberries, thawed
8-oz. pkg. frozen blueberries, thawed

Stir together water, sugar, corn syrup and cornstarch; pour into a 2-quart saucepan. Cook over medium heat, stirring constantly, until mixture thickens. Remove saucepan from heat and stir in gelatin until dissolved. Fold in raspberries and blueberries; gently stir. Serve over pancakes or waffles. Makes 8 servings.

Comfort is...
The smell of autumn leaves burning.

Sweet Dreams Hot Chocolate

Sarah Lundin
Forest Grove, OR

This recipe has been handed down through my family for at least 3 generations. At first glance it seems rather simple but it is in fact a magical concoction!

1 c. milk
chocolate syrup to taste
1/4 t. cinnamon

1/2 t. vanilla extract
Garnish: mini marshmallows

Warm milk in saucepan on low, taking care not to burn or scorch. As milk is warming, stir in chocolate syrup, cinnamon and vanilla with a small whisk or spoon. Do not beat the mixture, as it tends to foam and bubble. When ingredients have dissolved, remove from heat and pour into your favorite mug; top with marshmallows. Makes one serving.

Comfort is...
Cocoa with extra marshmallows.

A wonderful way to begin your day

Homemade Cinnamon Buns

Brandi Grosso
Springfield, PA

Simply delicious!

6 to 7-3/4 c. all-purpose flour, divided
2 pkgs. instant yeast
1-1/2 t. salt
1 c. plus 6 T. sugar, divided
1 c. milk

3/4 c. water
1/3 c. plus 4 T. butter, divided
3 eggs
1 c. brown sugar, packed
1 T. cinnamon

In a saucepan, mix 6 cups flour, yeast, salt and 6 tablespoons sugar together. In a separate saucepan over medium heat, bring milk, water and 1/3 cup butter to 120 degrees. Mix eggs into flour mixture one at a time. Slowly add milk mixture to flour mixture; mix for one minute and add 1-1/2 cups flour, 1/2 cup at time until dough is no longer sticky. Divide dough in half, roll each half in a 15"x9" rectangle and brush each half with 2 tablespoons butter. To prepare filling, blend together remaining sugar, brown sugar, 1/4 cup flour and cinnamon. Place filling evenly on each dough half and roll tightly, jelly roll-style beginning at the wide side. Using a sharp knife, or lengths of dental floss wrapped around the roll, cut in one to 1/2-inch slices. Place in a greased 13"x9" pan, let rise 30 to 40 minutes. Bake at 350 degrees for 15 minutes. Makes about 3 dozen cinnamon rolls.

Icing:

1/4 c. butter
3 8-oz. pkgs. cream cheese

1/2 c. powdered sugar
1/2 t. vanilla extract

Mix all ingredients together until smooth. Drizzle over warm cinnamon rolls.

Comfort is...
Your favorite pair of slippers.

Cider Coffee

Marlene Jorgensen
West Fulton, NY

Perfect for a chilly autumn day!

1/4 c. brown sugar, packed
1 c. apple juice
1/4 c. coffee granules

1/4 t. cinnamon
3 c. cold water

Using a coffee maker, place brown sugar and apple juice in coffee pot. Line the inside basket with a coffee filter and spoon in coffee and cinnamon. Add water to coffee maker and brew as usual. When finished brewing, stir until everything is well mixed. Makes 6 servings.

Comfort is...
Morning coffee with a friend.

A wonderful way to begin your day

Banana Crunch Coffee Cake

Cindy Watson
Gooseberry Patch

Serve with a tall glass of milk...mmm!

1-1/4 c. all-purpose flour
3/4 c. sugar
1 t. baking powder
1/4 t. baking soda
5 T. chilled butter, sliced
1/4 c. milk

1 banana, mashed and divided
1 egg
1 t. vanilla extract
1/2 c. flaked coconut
3 T. butter, melted

Whisk together flour, sugar, baking powder and baking soda; cut in butter. Blend together milk, 1/2 of the banana, egg and vanilla, then make a well in the center of flour mixture. Add milk mixture and gently stir until dry ingredients are moistened. Line a 9"x9" pan with aluminum foil, leaving a 2-inch overhang on 2 opposite sides. Spoon in batter and smooth with the back of a spoon. Bake at 375 degrees for 20 to 25 minutes or until center tests done. Remove from oven and cool completely on a wire rack; do not turn off oven. Mix together remaining banana, coconut and butter until well blended. Spread topping evenly over top of warm cake, return cake to oven and bake an additional 5 minutes or until topping is lightly golden. Cool baking dish on a wire rack for 10 minutes, then, using the overhanging foil as handles, lift cake from pan. Let cool completely before serving. Makes 16 servings.

Comfort is...
A homemade treat fresh from the oven.

Scrambled Corn & Eggs

Mary Clinesmith
Buffalo, KS

This recipe was a dish my mother came up with during the Depression, when my parents were struggling farmers and nothing was wasted!

5 to 6 ears sweet corn
2 T. butter
1 onion, diced
1 green pepper, chopped

4 to 5 eggs
1/8 t. hot pepper sauce
salt and pepper to taste

Remove corn from cob and sauté in butter with onion and green pepper for about 5 minutes. Beat together eggs and hot pepper sauce; add to the corn mixture. Stir and cook until eggs are set; season with salt and pepper. Makes 4 to 6 servings.

Comfort is...
Fresh flowers, just because.

Golden Potato Cakes

Athena Colegrove
Big Springs, TX

A fantastic way to use leftover mashed potatoes!

1/2 to 1 c. oil
1 c. potatoes, peeled, cooked and
    mashed
1 egg

4-1/2 T. all-purpose flour
1/2 t. baking powder
1 t. salt
1/4 c. milk

Add enough oil to 12" skillet to measure 1/4-inch deep. Blend together potatoes, egg, flour, baking powder, salt and milk, then shape mixture in 6 to 8 small, flat cakes. Add potato cakes to hot oil and cook over medium heat until edges are golden and centers are set. Turn each potato cake, and brown on the second side; repeat with remaining potato cakes. Makes 4 to 6 servings.

Comfort is...
Coming home to your very happy dog.

Cinnamon Fried Apples

Shelley Turner
Boise, ID

Use apples fresh from your nearest farmers'
market for a heavenly treat!

1/3 c. butter
1/2 to 3/4 c. sugar
1 T. plus 1 t. cornstarch
1/4 to 1/2 t. cinnamon

1-1/2 c. water
4 apples, peeled, cored and
   halved

Melt butter in a 10" skillet over medium heat, stir in sugar, cornstarch and cinnamon; mix well. Stir in water and apples, and cook, covered, over medium heat for 12 to 15 minutes, or until apples are tender and sauce is thick. Spoon sauce over apples before serving. Makes 4 servings.

Comfort is...
   Homemade apple cider.

Caramel Sticky Buns

Kathy Grashoff
Ft. Wayne, IN

*This is a delicious and easy recipe. My boys
love it and request it often!*

1/4 c. butter, melted
1/4 c. brown sugar, packed
2 T. corn syrup
1/4 c. chopped pecans

1 T. sugar
1/2 t. cinnamon
10-oz. can refrigerated flaky
   biscuits

In a small bowl, combine butter, brown sugar, corn syrup and pecans; mix well. Spoon scant tablespoons of topping into 12 greased muffin cups. In a medium bowl, combine sugar and cinnamon; mix well. Separate dough into 10 biscuits. Cut each biscuit into 6 pieces. Toss pieces in sugar-cinnamon mixture. Place 5 coated pieces of dough in each of the muffin cups. Place pan on baking sheet to guard against spills. Bake at 375 degrees for 15 to 20 minutes or until golden brown. Cool in pan for one minute; invert onto wax paper. Serve warm. Makes 12 rolls.

Comfort is...
Relaxing by candlelight.

Hot Molasses Cider

Rita Morgan
Pueblo, CO

Perfect for sipping!

6 whole cloves
2 slices lemon
1 qt. apple cider

1/4 c. molasses
2-1/4 inch cinnamon stick
2 T. lemon juice

Insert cloves into lemon slices. In a medium saucepan, bring lemon slices, apple cider, molasses and cinnamon stick to a boil. Reduce heat and simmer for 10 minutes. Discard cinnamon stick. Stir in lemon juice; serve immediately. Makes 4 cups.

Pure CIDER

Comfort is...
Being best friends with your brothers and sisters.

Sausage Gravy & Biscuits

Janet Pastrick
Gooseberry Patch

My absolute favorite comfort food...whether it's breakfast, lunch or dinner!

1/2 c. all-purpose flour
2 lbs. ground sausage, browned
   and drained

4 c. milk
salt and pepper to taste

Sprinkle flour in with sausage stirring until dissolved. Gradually add milk, and cook over medium heat until thick and bubbly. Season with salt and pepper and serve over warm biscuits. Makes 10 to 12 servings.

Biscuits:

4 c. self-rising flour
2 T. sugar
3 T. baking powder

7 T. shortening
2 c. buttermilk

Sift together flour, sugar and baking powder; cut in shortening. Mix in buttermilk with a fork, just until dough is moistened. Shape dough in a ball and knead a few times on a lightly floured surface. Roll out to 3/4-inch thickness and cut with a 3-inch biscuit cutter. Place biscuits on a greased baking sheet. Bake at 450 degrees for about 15 minutes or until golden. Makes 2 dozen biscuits.

Comfort is...
   Making a flower crown out of daisies.

Quilter's Tea

Shan Thiel
Saskatchewan, Canada

A wonderful, warm-your-tummy kind of tea.

5 teabags
2 cinnamon sticks
8 whole allspice
zest from 1/2 an orange
11 c. water

12-oz. can frozen orange juice
  concentrate
1/2 c. lemon juice
3/4 c. sugar
1/3 c. honey

In a cheesecloth bag, place teabags, cinnamon sticks, allspice and orange zest. Place bag in a 3-quart saucepan, add water and simmer for 10 minutes. Add remaining ingredients and simmer for an additional minute. Remove spice bag and serve. Makes 20 servings.

Comfort is...
Warm tea first thing in the morning.

A Wonderful way to beGiN your day

Creamed Country Ham

Nancy Wise
Little Rock, AR

Serve over warm cornbread for a warm and satisfying meal.

3 T. butter
3 T. onion, minced
3 T. green pepper, chopped
3 T. all-purpose flour

1-1/2 to 2 c. milk
1 c. cooked ham, chopped
1 T. fresh parsley, chopped
1/8 t. paprika

In a skillet, melt butter over medium heat and sauté the onion and green pepper until golden brown. Sprinkle in the flour and stir for a few minutes. Add milk slowly, stirring occasionally. Add ham and simmer, stirring until thickened. Remove pan from heat and season with remaining ingredients. Serve over cornbread. Makes 4 to 6 servings.

Cornbread:

3/4 c. cornmeal
2-1/4 c. all-purpose flour
1/2 c. sugar
3 t. baking powder

1 t. salt
1 c. buttermilk
1-1/2 sticks butter, melted
3 eggs, beaten

In a large bowl, mix together cornmeal, flour, sugar, baking powder and salt; blend well. Add buttermilk, butter and eggs; blend well. Pour into a greased and floured 13"x9" pan. Bake at 400 degrees for 20 minutes or until tested done. Makes 6 to 8 servings.

Comfort is...
Four generations of family together for a photo.

Fireside Coffee

*Sara Tschumper
Kenmore, WA*

*Store in a pretty jar tied with homespun and just add
boiling water when you need a pick me up.*

2 c. cocoa mix
2 c. non-dairy creamer
1 c. instant coffee granules

1 t. cinnamon
1/2 t. nutmeg
1-1/2 c. sugar

Blend cocoa mix, creamer, coffee, cinnamon and nutmeg in a blender;
add sugar. Place 4 teaspoons of mixture in your favorite mug and add
one cup boiling water. Makes 7 to 8 one cup servings.

*Comfort is...
A long and lazy summer day.*

A Wonderful way to begin your day

Russian Tea

Wendy Paffenroth
Pine Island, NY

A favorite with the college kids in the winter when studying!

1-1/4 c. orange drink mix
1 c. sweetened iced tea mix
1/2 t. cinnamon

1/4 t. ground cloves
1/8 t. salt, optional

Combine all ingredients together and place in a jar or other tightly covered container. When ready to serve, place one to 2 heaping teaspoons in a mug and fill with boiling water; stir until dissolved. Serve hot. Makes approximately 20 to 25 servings.

Comfort is...
Laughter in the air!

Morning Glory Muffins

Grace Keefe
Needham, MA

This is my favorite muffin recipe!

2-1/2 c. sugar
4 c. all-purpose flour
4 t. cinnamon
4 t. baking soda
1 t. salt
4 c. carrots, shredded
1 c. chopped walnuts

1 c. raisins
1 c. flaked coconut
6 eggs, beaten
1 c. applesauce
1 c. oil
1 t. vanilla extract

In a large bowl, using a wire whisk, blend sugar, flour, cinnamon, baking soda and salt. Add carrots, walnuts, raisins and coconut; mix well. Add remaining ingredients, stirring until well blended. Spoon batter into 2 dozen greased muffin cups. Bake at 350 degrees for about 20 minutes or until muffins are browned and test done. Makes 24 muffins.

Comfort is...
Baking a basket full of muffins to share.

Blueberry Jam Muffins

Becca Brasfield
Burns, TN

You can use any flavor jam or preserves, but the blueberry and banana tastes great together!

1 c. all-purpose flour
1/4 c. sugar
3/4 t. baking powder
1/8 t. baking soda
1/8 t. salt
4 T. butter, melted

1/2 c. sour cream
1 egg
1/2 t. vanilla extract
1 banana, mashed
1 to 2 T. milk
1/2 c. blueberry jam

Mix dry ingredients together in a bowl. Stir in butter, sour cream, egg, vanilla and banana. Add a little milk if batter seems too thick. Spoon batter into 10 to 12 greased muffin cups about 1/2 full. Drop one teaspoon of jam into the middle of each muffin. Bake at 400 degrees for 12 to 15 minutes. Cool slightly before removing from pan. Makes 10 to 12 muffins.

Comfort is...
Cross-country skiing on a moonlit night.

Raspberry Scones

Marlene Darnell
Newport Beach, CA

These scones are always a hit with overnight guests!

2 c. all-purpose flour
1/4 c. plus 1 T. sugar, divided
2-1/2 t. baking powder
1/4 t. salt
1/8 t. nutmeg
1 stick chilled butter, sliced

1/2 c. milk
1 egg
1 t. lemon zest
3/4 c. raspberries
1 T. butter, melted

Sift together flour, 1/4 cup sugar, baking powder, salt and nutmeg. Cut in chilled butter until mixture resembles coarse crumbs; set aside. In a separate bowl, combine milk, egg and lemon zest; stir into dry ingredients. When ingredients are thoroughly moistened and mixture forms a soft dough, fold in raspberries. Shape dough into a ball and knead gently on a lightly floured surface 8 to 10 times. Lightly coat a baking sheet with non-stick vegetable spray, then place dough in the center. Pat into a 9-inch circle about 1/2-inch thick. With a sharp knife, cut dough into 8 pie-shaped wedges; do not separate. Brush tops of dough with melted butter and sprinkle with remaining sugar. Bake scones at 425 degrees for 15 minutes or until golden brown. Cool on a wire rack. Makes 8 servings.

Comfort is...
Fresh-picked berries from your own backyard.

A wonderful way to begin your day...

Mountaintop Bacon

Wendy Jacobs
Idaho Falls, ID

This recipe was shared with me by my aunt in
West Virginia...a family favorite!

1/2 c. all-purpose flour
1/4 c. brown sugar, packed

1 t. pepper
1 lb. thickly sliced bacon

Mix flour, sugar and pepper together; sprinkle on bacon slices.
Place bacon on a baking sheet, then bake at 400 degrees for
10 to 15 minutes or until browned and crisp. Makes 4 to 6 servings.

Baked Oatmeal

Darlene Hartzler
Marshallville, OH

The perfect comfort dish.

2 eggs, beaten
1 c. milk
1/2 c. oil
1 c. brown sugar, packed
2 t. baking powder

1 t. salt
1 t. cinnamon
3 c. quick-cooking oats,
   uncooked

Mix all ingredients together with mixer. Pour into a lightly greased
13"x9" baking pan. Bake at 350 degrees for 25 to 30 minutes. Do
not let brown. Makes 6 to 8 servings.

Comfort is...
Running into an old friend.

Buttermilk Doughnuts

Jason Keller
Carrollton, GA

The fudge frosting is my favorite part!

2 c. potatoes, hot and mashed
2-1/2 c. sugar
2 c. buttermilk
2 eggs, beaten
2 T. butter, melted
2 t. baking soda

2 t. baking powder
1 t. nutmeg
1/2 t. salt
6-1/2 to 7 c. all-purpose flour
oil

Blend together potatoes, sugar, buttermilk and eggs in a large mixing bowl. Stir in butter, baking soda, baking powder, nutmeg, salt and enough flour until a soft dough forms. Place dough on a lightly floured surface and pat out to 3/4-inch thickness. Using a 2-1/2" floured doughnut cutter, cut out dough; repeat with any dough scraps. Add enough oil to an electric skillet to equal one inch. Heat oil to 375 degrees, add doughnuts and cook for 2 minutes on each side or until golden brown. Repeat with remaining doughnuts. Place on a paper towel-lined plate to cool until warm; frost if desired. Makes 4 dozen.

Frosting:

1 lb. powdered sugar
1/2 c. cocoa
1/4 t. salt

1/3 c. boiling water
1/3 c. butter, melted
1 t. vanilla extract

Sift together powdered sugar, cocoa and salt; stir in water, butter and vanilla. Spread frosting over warm doughnuts.

Comfort is...
A walk in the rain with a big umbrella.

Frosty Orange Juice

Kara Kimerline
Galion, OH

*My mom always made this for us on special days, like Christmas,
snow days or Sunday brunches. It is so refreshing!*

1 c. orange juice
1/2 t. vanilla extract
1/4 c. sugar

1/2 c. milk
4 to 5 ice cubes

Blend all ingredients together in a blender. Makes one serving.

Old-Fashioned Grape Juice

Barbara Tuve
Montvale, NJ

*This makes a serving of delicious homemade grape juice.
To make more, just double or triple the recipe!*

1 c. concord grapes
1/3 c. sugar

1 qt. boiling water

Place grapes and sugar into a quart-size canning jar. Fill jar with
boiling water, leaving about 1/2 inch space at top of jar. Secure jar lid
and tighten down ring. Process jar in a hot water bath for 30 minutes.
Strain juice before serving. Makes one serving.

gravy

Comforting
Suppers
&
Sides

FRESH iNGReDieNts
& a DASH of
TRADITION come
togetHer to
CReate
famiLy-frieNDLy
feasts

Creamed Chicken & Mushrooms

Tammy McCartney
Oxford, OH

This is one of those hearty meals best served with mashed potatoes, green beans and big, fluffy biscuits!

6 T. butter
6 T. all-purpose flour
1 t. salt
1/8 t. pepper
10-1/2 oz. can chicken broth

12-oz. can evaporated milk
1 to 2 c. cooked chicken, chopped
4-oz. can mushrooms, drained
1/4 c. white wine

In a 4-quart saucepan, melt butter and add flour, salt and pepper. Remove from heat and stir in broth and evaporated milk. Bring to a boil for one minute, stirring constantly. Stir in chicken, mushrooms and wine; heat through. Makes 6 to 8 servings.

Comfort is...
Sunday supper with the whole family.

Shepherd's Pie

Victoria Layser
Newmanstown, PA

There is nothing more comforting than a big slice of shepherd's pie.

1-1/2 lbs. ground beef, browned
15-oz. can tomato sauce
15-1/4 oz. can peas

4 c. potatoes, peeled, cooked and
   mashed
2 T. butter, sliced
1 T. paprika

Combine ground beef with tomato sauce. Place in a 2-quart casserole dish. Layer on peas, then top with potatoes. Dot with butter and sprinkle with paprika. Bake at 325 degrees for 30 to 45 minutes or until heated through. Makes 4 servings.

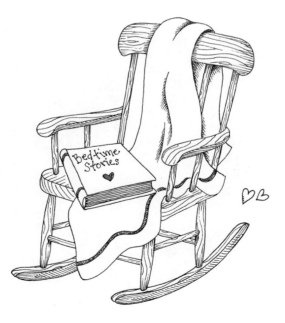

Comfort is...
Seeing joy in the eyes of children.

Garden-Fresh Green Beans

Courtney Anderson
Austin, MN

*Try wrapping these in an aluminum foil pouch and
placing on the grill. They taste wonderful!*

1/2 onion, sliced
4 slices bacon, crisply cooked
   and sliced, drippings
   reserved

2 lbs. green beans, snapped
2 carrots, thinly sliced
3/4 c. water
salt and pepper to taste

Sauté onions in bacon drippings. Add bacon, beans, carrots and water.
Cook on medium high for 25 to 30 minutes. Season with salt and
pepper. Makes 6 servings.

Comfort is...
   Rain on your rooftop in the
   middle of the night.

Candied Yams

Tina Stidam
Marengo, OH

These yams are a yummy addition to any meal!

3 to 4 lbs. yams, peeled and
   cubed
3/4 c. brown sugar, packed
4 T. butter, melted
1-1/2 t. cinnamon
1/4 t. nutmeg

2 T. orange juice
3 T. brandy
1-1/2 t. orange zest
1 c. mini marshmallows
1/2 c. chopped pecans, toasted

Place yams in a 4-quart slow cooker. In medium bowl, mix together brown sugar, butter, cinnamon, nutmeg and orange juice; spoon over yams. Cover and cook on low heat for 5 to 6 hours or until yams are tender, stirring only once. Stir in brandy and orange zest. Sprinkle the marshmallows and pecans over the top. Cover and cook 5 minutes longer, or until marshmallows are melted. Makes 8 to 12 servings.

Comfort is...
   planting your very own herb garden.

Ham & Noodle Casserole

Linda Charles
Oconomowoc, WI

Leftover ham is perfect for this dish!

1 onion, finely chopped
4 T. butter, melted
2 eggs, beaten
1 c. sour cream

1/2 c. Swiss cheese
1-1/2 c. cooked ham, chopped
salt to taste
1/2 lb. egg noodles, cooked

Sauté onion in butter over medium heat until soft. In a mixing bowl, combine the eggs and sour cream; add onion, cheese and ham. Season with salt. Place noodles into a buttered 2-quart casserole dish; add ham mixture and toss gently. Bake at 350 degrees for 45 minutes or until a straw inserted in the center comes out clean. Makes 6 to 8 servings.

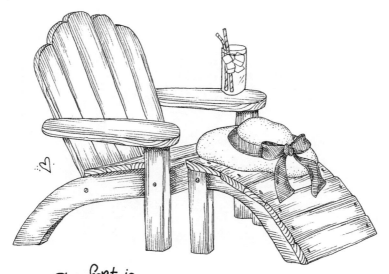

Comfort is...
The smell of fall in the late afternoon air.

Creamed Dried Beef

Diana Chaney
Olathe, KS

*Serve this tasty mixture over thickly sliced,
fresh-from-the-oven bread!*

1/4 lb. dried beef
4 T. butter
3 T. all-purpose flour

1 c. hot milk
1 c. light cream
1/4 t. pepper

Separate the dried beef slices; set aside. In a medium saucepan, melt butter until foamy, then sprinkle in flour. Stir mixture until well blended. Add milk and continue to cook over low heat, stirring frequently. Slowly blend in cream, stirring constantly until mixture thickens and is smooth. Add pepper and dried beef; stir and continue to heat until warmed throughout. Makes 4 servings.

There's No Place Like Home

Comfort is...
Washing dishes with the radio cranked up.

Sour Cream Potatoes

Stacey Keefer
Harveys Lake, PA

These are the perfect complement to your favorite meat loaf.

3/4 stick margarine
12-oz. pkg. sharp Cheddar
   cheese, cubed

8 potatoes, peeled, cooked and
   grated
12 oz. sour cream

In a saucepan, melt margarine and cheese over medium heat. In a large bowl, combine cheese mixture and potatoes; add sour cream. Pour into a 13"x9" pan. Bake at 350 degrees for 30 minutes or until heated through. Makes 6 to 8 servings.

Comfort is...
Finding a letter in your mailbox from that someone special you've been thinking about.

Chicken-Cornbread Dressing

Sandra Dodson
Indianapolis, IN

*This recipe is an old family favorite, passed down
from my mother-in-law, Joann!*

3-lb. chicken fryer
4 c. water
1/2 c. margarine, melted
1 t. salt, divided
1 t. pepper, divided
6 cubes chicken bouillon
4 c. sweet cornbread, crumbled

1 c. celery with leaves, chopped
2 10-oz. tubes refrigerated
   buttermilk biscuits, baked
   and torn
1 c. onion, finely chopped
1/2 t. dried sage

In a large Dutch oven, place chicken, water, margarine, 1/2 teaspoon salt, 1/2 teaspoon pepper and bouillon. Cover and simmer on medium heat for one hour, or until chicken is tender. Remove chicken to a platter to cool; reserve broth for dressing and set aside. Bone the chicken, tear into bite-size pieces and place in a bowl; set aside. In a separate bowl, mix together cornbread, celery, biscuits, onion, sage, remaining salt and pepper. Slowly add cooled chicken broth to cornbread mixture until desired consistency. Add chicken and pour mixture into a greased 13"x9" baking dish. Bake at 325 degrees for 1-1/2 hours. If needed during baking, add extra broth. Makes 8 to 10 servings.

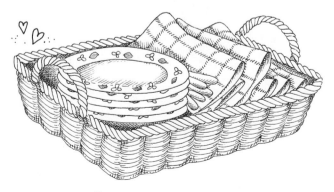

Comfort is...
Riding a bike!

Barbecued Honey Ham

Michelle Kasban
Overland, MO

*The sauce used in this recipe is also yummy used
as a ham glaze or over sliced roast beef!*

1 c. French honey-style salad
   dressing
1 c. catsup
1 c. apple butter

1/2 c. steak sauce
1 T. Worcestershire sauce
2 lbs. cooked ham, sliced
12 buns

In a large bowl, mix dressing, catsup, apple butter, steak sauce and
Worcestershire sauce together. Place ham into a 13"x9" casserole dish.
Pour sauce over ham. Bake at 350 degrees for 30 minutes. Serve on
buns. Makes 6 servings.

Pure
CLOVER
HONEY

Comfort is...
making a new friend.

Mashed Potato-Meat Loaf Casserole   *Jo Ann*

For another tasty version, try using ground chicken.

2 onions, chopped
1 T. oil
1 clove garlic, minced
1 t. dried oregano, crumbled
1/2 t. dried basil, crumbled
1 lb. ground beef
3 eggs, divided
1/2 c. bread crumbs
1/2 c. tomato sauce

1/4 c. fresh basil, chopped
1/4 c. chicken broth
1 T. cider vinegar
1-1/2 t. salt, divided
1/4 t. plus 1/8 t. pepper, divided
4 potatoes, peeled, cubed and
  cooked
1/2 c. sour cream
1 T. unsalted butter

Over medium heat, sauté onions in oil until tender. Stir in garlic, oregano and dried basil; continue to cook one minute longer. Spoon into a large bowl; set aside for 10 minutes. Crumble ground beef into onion mixture, add 2 eggs, bread crumbs, tomato sauce, fresh basil, broth, vinegar, one teaspoon salt and 1/4 teaspoon pepper. Thoroughly blend until mixture is combined. Shape into a loaf and place into an oiled 2-quart casserole dish. Using the palms of your hands or the back of a spatula, press beef mixture over bottom and up sides of casserole dish; set aside. Mash potatoes with sour cream, butter and remaining salt and pepper. Beat remaining egg, then fold into potato mixture; stirring until fluffy. Spoon potatoes into the center of meat loaf shell and bake at 350 degrees for 50 minutes to one hour or until potatoes are puffed and lightly golden brown. Let stand 15 minutes before serving. Makes 6 servings.

Comfort is...
   *Being with your children, going for a walk,
     sharing and laughing together.*

Baked Creamed Corn

Donna Nowicki
Center City, MN

This will be a well-loved addition to any meal!

2 eggs, beaten
1 c. milk
1 T. sugar
1 t. salt

2 T. butter
1/8 t. pepper
1 c. cream-style corn
1/4 c. Cheddar cheese, grated

In a large bowl, combine eggs, milk, sugar, salt, butter, pepper and corn; mix well. Pour into a greased 2-quart baking dish. Sprinkle cheese over the top. Bake at 350 degrees for 30 minutes. Makes 3 servings.

Comfort is...
A picnic lunch on a sunny day.

Stuffing 'n Tomatoes

Patricia Nuernberg
Scottsdale, AZ

Try substituting your favorite seasoned croutons for the stuffing mix!

1/3 c. butter
1/2 to 1 t. salt
1 t. fresh basil leaves, crumbled
1/4 t. pepper
1/2 c. celery, sliced

1/2 c. green pepper, sliced
1/4 c. onion, chopped
1 c. seasoned stuffing mix
4 tomatoes, coarsely chopped
2 t. sugar

In a heavy 10" skillet, melt butter and add seasonings. Sauté celery, green pepper and onion, uncovered, in butter mixture over medium high heat until crisp-tender. Add stuffing; toss. Add tomatoes and sugar; toss gently. Cover and continue cooking about 10 to 12 minutes or until tomatoes are hot but firm. Makes 4 to 5 servings.

Comfort is...
The arrival of the first robin to tell us spring has sprung.

Flaky Beef Turnovers

Kay Marone
Des Moines, IA

My family loves it when I bake this dish...it's so tasty!

6-oz. boneless ribeye steak, cubed
2 potatoes, peeled and diced
3 T. dry onion soup mix

2 T. catsup
1 t. Worcestershire sauce
1 T. fresh parsley, chopped
10-oz. pkg. puff pastry shells

In a large bowl, stir together steak, potatoes, onion soup mix, catsup, Worcestershire sauce and parsley. On a lightly floured surface, roll out each pastry shell into a 7-inch circle. Fill each pastry circle with approximately 1/4 cup of meat mixture, then lightly brush pastry edges with water. Fold circles in half and seal edges with tines of a fork. Cut several slits in the tops of each turnover to vent the steam and place on a lightly greased baking sheet. Bake at 400 degrees for 20 to 25 minutes or until golden brown. Makes 6 turnovers.

Comfort is...
Stepping on the scale and it's down a pound!

Homestyle Stroganoff

Wendy Paffenroth
Pine Island, NY

Serve this dish with a nice green salad, coleslaw
or homegrown vegetables!

1/2 to 3/4 c. all-purpose flour
1/8 t. salt
1/8 t. pepper
1/8 t. paprika
1/8 t. garlic powder
2 lbs. stew meat
oil
2 c. chicken broth

4 onions, quartered
8-oz. pkg. fresh mushrooms,
    quartered
1 cube beef bouillon
1 c. warm water
16-oz. pkg. wide egg noodles,
    uncooked
1/2 c. sour cream onion dip

In a large plastic zipping bag, place flour, salt, pepper, paprika and garlic powder. Shake bag until evenly mixed. Add stew meat and shake to coat. In a heavy Dutch oven, coat the bottom with oil. Remove meat from flour mixture and brown meat in oil; remove. Add chicken bouillon to the drippings; place onions and mushrooms in Dutch oven. Add beef and beef bouillon; bring to a boil, stirring often. Reduce to a simmer. Prepare egg noodles according to package directions and when the egg noodles are ready, turn off the stroganoff and add onion dip to the gravy. Stir in, but do not boil. Makes 4 servings.

Comfort is...
Homegrown tomatoes still
warm from the vine.

Creamy Macaroni & Cheese

Liz Brady
Manchester, NH

The spicy brown mustard gives this a little kick!

6 T. butter, divided
3 T. all-purpose flour
2 c. milk
8-oz. pkg. cream cheese, cubed
2 c. Cheddar cheese, shredded
2 t. spicy brown mustard

1/2 t. salt
1/4 t. pepper
7 oz. elbow macaroni, cooked
3/4 c. bread crumbs
2 T. fresh parsley, minced

Melt 4 tablespoons butter in a large saucepan. Stir in flour until smooth. Gradually add milk; bring to a boil. Cook and stir for 2 minutes. Reduce heat, add cheeses, mustard, salt and pepper. Stir until cheese is melted and sauce is smooth. Add macaroni to cheese sauce; stir to coat. Transfer to a 3-quart baking dish. In a separate saucepan, melt the remaining butter and toss with bread crumbs and parsley; sprinkle over macaroni. Bake, uncovered, at 400 degrees for 15 to 20 minutes or until golden brown. Makes 6 to 8 servings.

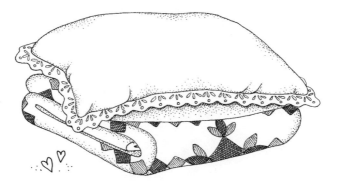

Comfort is...
Clean, crisp sheets and a cozy quilt.

Parmesan Baked Tomatoes

Tori Willis
Champaign, IL

*This is super in the summer when you have
fresh-from-the-garden tomatoes!*

3/4 c. bread crumbs
3 T. grated Parmesan cheese
2 T. olive oil, divided

1 t. garlic, minced
5 tomatoes

Stir together bread crumbs, Parmesan cheese, one tablespoon olive oil and garlic. Using a sharp knife, slice the top 1/3 from each tomato and place cut side up in an 11"x7" baking dish. Divide bread crumb mixture equally among each tomato and sprinkle over tomato tops. Drizzle tops with remaining olive oil, then bake at 450 degrees for 8 to 10 minutes or until bread crumbs are toasted. Makes 5 servings.

Comfort is...
Walking barefoot on cool, freshly-clipped grass.

Grandma's Ham Loaf

Beth Goblirsch
Minneapolis, MN

*This was always a part of our traditional Christmas Eve
dinner with my mother's side of the family.*

2-1/2 lbs. ground ham
2 lbs. ground beef
1 lb. ground pork
3 eggs

2 8-oz. cans tomato sauce
salt and pepper to taste
1 c. round buttery crackers,
   crumbled

Mix all ingredients thoroughly together. Shape into 2 loaves and
place in 2 lightly greased 9"x5" loaf pans. Bake at 350 degrees for
1-1/2 hours. Makes 16 servings.

*Comfort is...
Mashed potatoes and gravy.*

Salisbury Steak

Tammy McCartney
Oxford, OH

This is one of those great, warm comfort foods.
Serve with mashed potatoes and a salad.

1 lb. ground chuck
1/2 c. bread crumbs
1/2 c. onion, finely chopped
1 egg
1-1/2 t. salt, divided
1/4 t. pepper, divided

1/8 t. allspice
1/2 lb. fresh mushrooms, sliced
1-1/2 c. water
3 T. all-purpose flour
1 T. catsup

In a large bowl, combine ground chuck, bread crumbs, onion, egg,
1/2 teaspoon salt, 1/8 teaspoon pepper and allspice. Shape into 4 oval
patties. Sauté beef patties in oil for 3 to 5 minutes per side. Remove
from oil and keep warm. Add mushrooms to skillet; sauté until
golden. In small bowl, gradually beat water into flour. Stir into
mushroom mixture along with catsup and remaining salt and pepper.
Makes 4 servings.

Comfort is...
gooshing mud between your toes!

Au Gratin Potatoes

Donna Walker
Evansville, IN

Make these ahead of time and freeze for a last-minute addition to any meal.

8 to 10 potatoes, boiled, peeled
   and diced
1/2 t. salt
1/8 t. pepper
8 T. butter

4 T. all-purpose flour
2 c. milk
1 lb. pasteurized process cheese
   spread, cubed and divided

Place potatoes in an ungreased 13"x9" baking pan; season with salt and pepper. Melt butter in saucepan and add flour; stir. Add milk and bring to a boil, stirring constantly. When mixture starts to thicken, add 3/4 of cheese. Pour sauce mixture over potatoes; mix thoroughly. Let potatoes and sauce sit for for 15 minutes. Grate remaining cheese on top. Bake at 350 degrees for 40 to 50 minutes or until hot and cheese on top is slightly brown. Makes 10 to 12 servings.

Comfort is...
Bird watching on a park bench.

Broccoli-Cheddar Casserole

Caroline Talmage
LaGrange, IN

A side dish that everyone can agree on!

8 c. broccoli, chopped
1 c. onion, finely chopped
2 T. butter
12 eggs
2 c. whipping cream

2 c. Cheddar cheese, shredded
  and divided
2 t. salt
1 t. pepper

In a skillet, over medium heat, sauté broccoli and onion in butter for about 5 minutes or until crisp-tender; set aside. In a large bowl, beat eggs. Add whipping cream and 1-3/4 cups cheese; mix well. Stir in the broccoli mixture, salt and pepper. Pour into a greased 3-quart baking dish; set into a larger pan filled with one inch of hot water. Bake, uncovered, at 350 degrees for 45 to 50 minutes or until knife comes out clean. Sprinkle with remaining cheese, let stand for 10 minutes before serving. Makes 12 to 16 servings.

Stop and smell ♥ the roses

Comfort is...
A bouquet of roses you've tended yourself.

Chicken & Dumplings

Sandy Dodson
Indianapolis, IN

This recipe took me years of trial and error, but lo, and behold I finally got it right! My husband, children and granddaughters say that these are they best they have ever eaten.

2 to 3-lb. chicken
4 c. water
6 cubes chicken bouillon
2 T. margarine
1-1/4 t. salt, divided
1-1/4 t. pepper, divided

2 stalks celery, sliced
2 carrots, thinly sliced
2 c. all-purpose flour
1 t. dried, chopped chives, divided
1/2 to 1 c. chicken broth

Thoroughly rinse chicken and place in a Dutch oven. Add water, bouillon cubes, margarine, one teaspoon salt and one teaspoon pepper. Bring to a boil; reduce to simmer. Add celery and carrots; continue to cook for one hour or until chicken is tender. Remove chicken from broth and bone; set aside. Continue simmering broth. In a mixing bowl, combine flour, 1/2 teaspoon chives, remaining salt and pepper. Slowly add chicken broth to form dough. Knead dough for 5 minutes, then pour the dough mixture onto a floured cutting board. Roll dough out to 1/4-inch thickness and cut into squares. Add remaining chives to simmering broth; add dumplings one at a time until all dumplings are in the Dutch oven. Cover and simmer for 45 minutes then add chicken; continue to simmer for an additional 20 minutes. Makes 6 servings.

Comfort is...
a good book on a quiet evening.

Pork Chops Supreme

Sharon Pawlak
Castle Rock, CO

*These pork chops are terrific served with rice,
mashed potatoes or pasta.*

6 pork chops
paprika to taste
salt to taste
pepper to taste
2 T. olive oil
1 c. water

1/2 c. celery, chopped
1-1/2 oz. dry onion soup mix
2 T. all-purpose flour
1 T. fresh parsley, chopped
1/4 c. cold water
6-oz. can evaporated milk

Season pork chops with paprika, salt and pepper. Brown pork chops slowly in hot oil; drain off excess oil. Add water, celery and onion soup mix. Cover and cook over low heat for 45 minutes, or until pork chops are tender. Remove pork chops from pan and place on a platter. In a small bowl, combine flour, parsley and cold water; mix until smooth. Blend into pan drippings, adding evaporated milk. Cook and stir until sauce is thick and bubbly, about 2 to 3 minutes. Cover pork chops with sauce. Makes 6 servings.

Comfort is...
*The time of day when the sun is just about to set,
casting long, dark shadows.*

Twice-Baked Potatoes

Mary Bettuchy
Duxbury, MA

This tried-and-true recipe is a cinch!

4 potatoes, baked
1/3 c. butter
1/3 to 1/2 c. milk

1/4 t. paprika
12 slices bacon, crisply cooked
   and crumbled

Cut potatoes in half lengthwise and scoop potato out of skins into a medium mixing bowl. Mash in butter and milk as necessary to make potatoes slightly creamy; stir in paprika. Spoon potato mixture back into the potato skins, dividing mixture evenly between all 8 skins. Place skins on a baking sheet and bake at 425 degrees for 10 minutes, or until potato mixture gets slightly brown on top. When potatoes are done, crumble bacon over each potato. Makes 8 servings.

Comfort is...
   Brand new fuzzy socks!

Sweet Potato Pudding

Carolyn Celeste
Brick, NJ

This recipe has been in my family as long as I can remember!
Every holiday, I get requests to bring this pudding.

10 sweet potatoes, baked, peeled
   and mashed
3/4 c. brown sugar, packed
1/2 c. butter

4 eggs, beaten
3/4 to 1 c. light cream
1 t. cinnamon

Place potatoes in a large bowl, beat in brown sugar and butter; mix well. Blend in eggs, cream and cinnamon. Whip until well blended; pour into a 5-quart casserole dish. Bake at 350 degrees for 30 to 40 minutes or until heated through. Makes 10 to 12 servings.

Comfort is...
Seeing someone's face light up after you've
given them a present.

Slow Cooker Turkey & Dressing

*Geneva Rogers
Gillette, WY*

*I like to start this before I leave for work...I just need
to slice and serve when I get home!*

8-oz. pkg. stuffing mix
1/2 c. hot water
2 T. butter, softened
1 onion, chopped
1/2 c. celery, chopped

1/4 c. sweetened, dried
   cranberries
3-lb. boneless turkey breast
1/4 t. dried basil
1/2 t. salt
1/2 t. pepper

Coat a 4-quart slow cooker with non-stick vegetable spray; spoon in
dry stuffing mix. Add water, butter, onion, celery and cranberries; mix
well. Sprinkle turkey breast with basil, salt and pepper and place over
stuffing mixture. Cook on low, covered, for 6 to 7 hours. Remove
turkey, slice and set aside. Gently stir the stuffing and allow to sit for
5 minutes. Transfer stuffing to a platter and top with sliced turkey.
Makes 4 to 6 servings.

Comfort is...
*Watching flickering fireflies on a
quiet summer evening.*

Best Meat Loaf

Marian Collins
Mission Viejo, CA

Makes great sandwiches the next day!

4 lbs. ground beef
4 eggs, beaten
2 10-1/2 oz. cans onion soup
8-oz. pkg. cornbread flavored
  stuffing mix

1 t. salt
1 c. catsup
1/4 t. dry mustard
1/4 c. cider vinegar
1/2 c. brown sugar, packed

Combine ground beef, eggs, onion soup, stuffing mix and salt. Divide into thirds; form each into a loaf. Place loaves into a 13"x9" baking pan. Bake at 350 degrees for one to 1-1/2 hours or until well browned. In a medium bowl, mix together remaining ingredients; set aside. Drain juices off meat loaves and top with brown sugar mixture. Bake an additional 30 minutes. Makes 16 servings.

Comfort is...
*A homecooked meal and a cold shower
after a hot day of baling hay.*

Creamy Mashed Potatoes

Erin Dempsey-Perry
Rumford, RI

A simple, yet tasty side dish!

8 to 10 potatoes, peeled and
    halved
8-oz. pkg. cream cheese
8 oz. sour cream

1/2 c. butter
1/4 c. chives, chopped
1-1/2 t. salt
paprika to taste

Cook potatoes in boiling water about 30 minutes or until tender; drain and mash. In a large bowl, beat cream cheese with mixer until smooth. Add potatoes, sour cream, butter, chives and salt. Spoon into a buttered 2-quart casserole dish; sprinkle top with paprika. Bake, uncovered, at 350 degrees for 30 minutes or until warm throughout. Makes 8 to 10 servings.

Comfort is...
A brand new box of crayons!

Celery & Onion Stuffing

Kerry Mayer
Dunham Springs, LA

This is so easy to make and I always get tons of compliments.

1-lb. dry stuffing mix
10-3/4 oz. can cream of
   mushroom soup

10-3/4 oz. cream of chicken
   soup
1 c. onion, chopped
1 c. celery, chopped

In a large mixing bowl, stir together stuffing mix, soups, one to 1-1/2 soup cans of water, onion and celery. Place stuffing mixture into a greased 11"x7" casserole dish. Bake, covered with aluminum foil, at 325 degrees for 10 minutes. Remove foil and continue to bake for 50 minutes or until top is golden. Makes 6 servings.

Comfort is...
   Autumn leaves gently falling to the ground.

Easy Beef Barbecue

Sharon Goss
Beech Grove, IN

This is a great recipe to start in the morning...it's ready by the time you get home from work!

4-lb. chuck roast
1 onion, chopped
1 green pepper, chopped
2 stalks celery
17-oz. bottle catsup
1 T. vinegar

3 T. barbecue sauce
1/4 t. hot pepper sauce
1/2 c. brown sugar, packed
1/2 t. cinnamon
12 Kaiser rolls

Layer ingredients, except for rolls, in a slow cooker as listed. Cook on low for 8 to 10 hours. Shred roast after cooking, spoon on Kaiser rolls. Makes 12 servings.

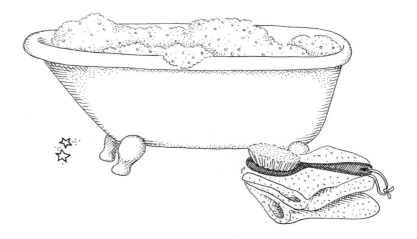

Comfort is...
A fragrant bubble bath after a long day.

Homemade Beef Casserole

Vickie Milillo
Schuylkill Haven, PA

*There's nothing better than this beef casserole on
a cold and snowy night!*

1 lb. elbow macaroni, cooked
1-1/2 lbs. ground beef, browned
8 oz. Cheddar cheese, shredded
· and divided

2 15-oz. cans tomato sauce,
   divided
1-1/8 t. zesty Italian spices,
   divided

In a large bowl, place macaroni, beef, all but one cup of cheese,
1-1/2 cans tomato sauce and one teaspoon Italian spices; pour
mixture into 13"x9" baking pan. Top with remaining 1/2 can
of tomato sauce and sprinkle with reserved cup of cheese. Sprinkle
with remaining Italian spices. Bake, covered with aluminum foil, at
350 degrees for about 30 to 45 minutes. Makes 6 servings.

Comfort is...
   Wind whistling through the trees.

Virginia's Baked Spaghetti

Mindy Beard
Yorktown, IN

This is my husband's grandma's recipe. She loved to bake and cook but rarely used a recipe...it came straight from her heart! I am so fortunate to have this one written down.

16-oz. pkg. spaghetti noodles, cooked
2 24-oz. jars spaghetti sauce
2 lbs. ground beef, browned
4 T. butter
4 T. all-purpose flour
4 T. grated Parmesan cheese
2 t. salt
1/2 t. garlic
12-oz. can evaporated milk
3 c. Cheddar cheese, shredded and divided

Combine spaghetti noodles, spaghetti sauce and ground beef together; set aside. In a saucepan, over medium heat, melt butter; add flour, Parmesan cheese, salt and garlic. Stir constantly over heat until smooth and bubbly. Add evaporated milk and one cup Cheddar cheese; stir until thoroughly melted. Pour half of the spaghetti noodle mixture into a 13"x9" casserole dish and pour cheese mixture over top. Pour remaining noodle mixture into casserole dish; top with remaining Cheddar cheese. Bake at 350 degrees for 25 to 30 minutes. Makes 12 to 18 servings.

Comfort is...
The smell of freshly-cut grass.

Marzetti

DeNeane Deskins
Marengo, OH

Top with mozzarella for a cozy supper!

1 lb. ground beef	Italian seasoning to taste
1 onion, chopped	1 bay leaf
1 green pepper, chopped	salt and pepper to taste
2 c. tomato sauce	1 lb. elbow macaroni, cooked
1 c. tomato paste	

Brown beef, onion and pepper together; drain. Add tomato sauce, tomato paste and seasonings. Combine macaroni and beef mixture; simmer for 5 to 10 minutes. Remove bay leaf. Serves 8 to 10.

Comfort is...
a garden in bloom.

Crunchy Biscuit Chicken

Mary Makulec
Rockford, IL

Chicken, beans, cheese and biscuits...what more could you want?

2 c. boneless, skinless chicken, cooked
10-3/4 oz. can cream of chicken soup
1 c. canned green beans, undrained
1 c. Cheddar cheese, shredded
1/4 c. canned mushrooms, undrained

1/2 c. mayonnaise-type salad dressing
1 t. lemon juice
10-oz. tube refrigerated flaky biscuits
1 to 2 T. margarine, melted
1/4 c. Cheddar cheese croutons, crushed

In a medium saucepan, combine chicken, soup, green beans, cheese, mushrooms, salad dressing and lemon juice; heat until hot and bubbly. Pour hot chicken mixture into an ungreased 13"x9" baking dish. Separate biscuit dough into 10 biscuits. Arrange biscuits over chicken mixture. Brush each biscuit with margarine; sprinkle with croutons. Bake at 375 degrees for 25 to 30 minutes or until deep, golden brown. Makes 4 to 6 servings.

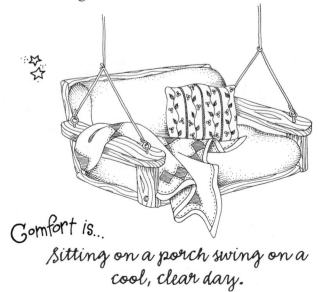

Comfort is...
Sitting on a porch swing on a cool, clear day.

Pork & Sauerkraut

Sherry Gordon
Arlington Heights, IL

This is my favorite dish to serve on those nights when the whole family is going in different directions. I start it in the morning and its ready to serve by the time I get home.

4 to 6 pork chops
2 c. sauerkraut, drained
1/2 head cabbage, shredded
4 potatoes, peeled and chopped

1/4 c. brown sugar, packed
10-1/2 oz. can beef broth
10-3/4 oz. can cream of
    mushroom soup

Mix all ingredients together in a slow cooker. Cook for 6 hours on high heat or until meat is tender. Makes 4 to 6 servings.

School Days Sloppy Joe's

Gina O'Connor
Lake Villa, IL

For a fun variation, try topping with Cheddar cheese and pickles!

1 lb. ground beef
1/2 onion, chopped
1/2 c. celery, chopped
1 c. catsup
1 t. ground mustard

1 T. vinegar
1 T. brown sugar, packed
1/4 c. water
1/2 t. chili seasoning
8 buns, sliced and toasted

Brown ground beef, onion and celery. Add next 6 ingredients and simmer for 20 minutes. Serve on buns. Makes 4 servings.

Comfort is...

* *Rocking a baby to sleep with an old-fashioned lullaby.*

B.

Hot Ham & Cheese Sandwiches

Nancy Molldrem
Eau Claire, WI

These tasty sandwiches are great for a crowd! Make ahead, place them in the refrigerator and pop them in the oven right before your company arrives.

1/4 lb. butter, softened
1/2 c. onion, chopped
1-1/2 T. mustard
1-1/2 T. poppy seeds

12 hamburger buns
12 slices cooked ham
12 slices Swiss cheese

Combine butter, onion, mustard and poppy seeds with a mixer. Spread on both halves of each bun. Place a slice of ham and cheese on each. Wrap each sandwich individually in aluminum foil. Bake at 350 degrees for 15 minutes. Makes 12 sandwiches.

Comfort is...
Flying a kite and letting a child hold the string.

Roast Beef with Vegetables

T.J. Riffle
Columbus, OH

When this comes out of the oven, it's ready to melt in your mouth.

3 to 5-lb. chuck roast
2 T. butter, melted
garlic to taste, minced and
    divided
3 onions, halved

6 to 8 redskin potatoes, halved
    or quartered
10 carrots, halved
fresh basil to taste

Sear both sides of roast in butter with a sprinkling of garlic; place roast in a large roasting pan. Place onions, cut side down, on roast. Place potatoes and carrots around the roast. Pour water into the pan until it just comes below the top of the meat. Sprinkle vegetables with additional garlic and basil. Bake, covered, at 350 degrees for one hour to 1-1/2 hours; reduce heat to 250 degrees and cook an additional 3 to 4 hours. Makes 4 to 6 servings.

Comfort is...
Your favorite meal.

Green Pepper Steak

Kendall Hale
Lynn, MA

My husband's favorite after a hard day!

1-lb. round steak
1/4 c. soy sauce
1 clove garlic, diced
1-1/2 t. fresh ginger, grated
1/4 c. oil
1 c. green onion, thinly sliced

1 c. green pepper, thinly sliced
1 stalk celery, thinly sliced
1 T. cornstarch
1 c. water
2 tomatoes, coarsely chopped

Cut steak across the grain into thin strips about 1/8-inch thick. Blend together soy sauce, garlic and ginger; add beef and toss. Add oil to a deep skillet, add steak and toss over high heat until browned. If meat is not tender, cover and simmer for 30 to 40 minutes over low heat until tender and browned. Turn heat up to medium-high, add green onion, pepper and celery. Stir until vegetables are crisp-tender, about 10 minutes. Blend together cornstarch and water until smooth; add to pan. Stir and cook until thickened; add tomatoes and heat through. Makes 4 servings.

Comfort is...
The smell of baking bread.

Apple-Pork Tenderloin

*Mary-Ellen Tillotson
Andover, MA*

This dish is wonderful served with mashed potatoes and acorn squash. Halve a baked squash and place the mashed potatoes in the center...yum!

3-lb. pork tenderloin
6 to 8 apples, peeled, cored and
   sliced
1 onion, chopped

1 t. cinnamon
2 T. sugar
1 c. apple cider
2 T. garlic, minced

Place pork in the center of a roasting pan. Combine apples, onion, cinnamon and sugar together and place in pan surrounding pork. Pour apple cider over the pork. Spread garlic over the top. Bake, uncovered, at 325 degrees for 1 to 1-1/2 hours or until pork is cooked. Makes 8 servings.

Comfort is...
Sleeping under the stars on a warm night.

Macaroni & Vegetable Bake

Samantha Starks
Madison, WI

My mother used to make this in the oven, but I've found the microwave version is just as tasty...only quicker!

16-oz. pkg. elbow macaroni,
   cooked
1 c. carrots, chopped and cooked
1 c. yellow squash, chopped and
   cooked
2 T. butter

2 T. all-purpose flour
1/4 t. pepper
1/4 t. dry mustard
1-1/2 c. milk
Garnish: Cheddar cheese, grated

Place macaroni into a 2-quart microwave-safe casserole dish. Blend together vegetables and macaroni; set aside. Combine butter, flour and pepper; microwave on high for one minute. Whisk in mustard and milk; microwave an additional 3 minutes. Whisk again and continue to microwave for one to 2 minutes or until mixture thickens. Blend with vegetables and sprinkle with cheese. Microwave an additional one to 2 minutes; serve. Makes 8 to 10 servings.

Comfort is...
   Cinnamon & sugar on your toast.

Farmer's Casserole

Lisa Burns
Findlay, OH

A hearty, homestyle meal!

3 c. frozen, shredded hash
 browns
3/4 c. Monterey Jack cheese,
 shredded
1 c. cooked ham, diced

1/4 c. green onions, chopped
4 eggs
12-oz. can evaporated milk
1/8 t. salt
1/4 t. pepper

Place hash browns in an 8"x8" baking dish. Sprinkle with cheese, ham and onions. In a mixing bowl, beat eggs, milk, salt and pepper together; pour over hash browns. Cover and refrigerate overnight. Remove from refrigerator 30 minutes before baking. Bake, uncovered, at 350 degrees for 55 minutes to one hour or until a knife inserted in the center comes out clean. Makes 6 servings.

Comfort is...
 Best friends, old memories and laughter.

Tomato Pie

Shelia Willis
Annapolis, MD

Grow your own tomatoes and basil this year and use them in this tasty tomato pie!

4 tomatoes, chopped
1 onion, chopped
10 to 12 leaves fresh basil,
   chopped
9-inch pie crust, baked

1 c. mozzarella cheese, shredded
1 c. Cheddar cheese, shredded
1 c. mayonnaise
1/2 c. grated Parmesan cheese

Layer half of tomato, onion and basil in pie crust; repeat layers. Mix mozzarella and Cheddar cheese with mayonnaise. Spread mixture over top of pie; top with Parmesan cheese. Bake at 350 degrees for 50 to 60 minutes. Let stand 15 minutes before cutting. Makes 6 servings.

Comfort is...
planting a garden.

Orange-Maple Glazed Carrots

Elizabeth Blackstone
Racine, WI

This dish always impresses guests...don't let them know you did it in the microwave.

2/3 c. orange juice
12 carrots, peeled and
   thinly sliced
zest of one orange

5 T. maple syrup
1 t. fresh nutmeg, grated
5 T. butter

Heat orange juice in a microwave-safe casserole dish in the microwave on high for 1-1/2 minutes. Add carrots and orange zest; stir to coat. Cover dish and microwave on high for 7 minutes. Stir in the remaining ingredients and microwave, uncovered, for 2 minutes. Carrots should be crisp-tender, if not, microwave an additional 2 minutes. Makes 3 to 4 servings.

Comfort is...
Shopping with your girlfriends.

Creamy Rice Pudding

Kathy Ann Majeski
Pittsburgh, PA

My Aunt Sis's speciality! Serve this at your next family gathering...you'll be sure to get a lot of praise.

1 c. rice, cooked
1/2 c. sugar
3 eggs, beaten
1 t. vanilla extract

12-oz. can evaporated milk
1/4 to 1/2 c. golden raisins
4 to 5 pats of butter

In a mixing bowl, place warm rice; add sugar, eggs and vanilla. Pour evaporated milk into a 4-cup measuring cup and add enough water to make 32-ounces of liquid. Add to rice mixture; blend in raisins. Pour rice mixture into a buttered 13"x9" baking dish; dot with butter. Bake at 350 degrees for 30 to 35 minutes or until liquid is set. Serve warm. Makes 15 to 18 servings.

Comfort is...
    The house is clean, laundry is done and you
        have the rest of the day to relax.

Warming Soups & Stews

Come in from the COLD to steamy, Soup simmering on the stove... So cozy, warm & comfy.

Hearty Beef Stew with Dumplings

Sandra Dodson
Indianapolis, IN

A fabulous dish to serve after your annual hayride!

1 lb. stew meat, chopped	1 T. browning sauce
2 T. oil	5 potatoes, coarsely chopped
1 onion, chopped	1 lb. baby carrots
1 clove garlic, minced	1-1/2 c. peas
4 c. water, divided	1 c. celery, chopped
1 t. dried chives	2 T. cornstarch
1/2 t. dried thyme	1-1/3 c. all-purpose flour
1/4 t. dried sage	1 T. baking powder
2 t. salt, divided	1 t. dried parsley
1/3 t. plus 1/4 t. pepper, divided	1 egg, beaten

In a large Dutch oven, brown stew meat in oil; add onion and garlic. Cook for about 20 minutes, or until onion is lightly browned and tender. Add 3 cups water, chives, thyme, sage, 1-1/2 teaspoon salt and 1/3 teaspoon pepper. Cover and simmer for 2-1/2 hours or until meat is tender. Add browning sauce, potatoes, carrots, peas and celery to mixture; simmer an additional 40 minutes or until vegetables are tender. In a mixing bowl, stir together cornstarch and slowly add 1/2 cup water to form a smooth consistency. Slowly stir cornstarch mixture into stew. Turn heat up to medium, cover and let simmer for 10 minutes. In a medium bowl, add flour, baking powder, parsley, remaining salt and pepper. Beat in egg and remaining water; stir until blended. Remove cover from stew and turn to medium high heat to light boiling stage. Drop dumpling mixture by tablespoon into boiling stew. Cover stew and continue cooking for 10 minutes. Makes 6 to 8 servings.

Comfort is...

Looking out the front window at a pasture of playful, sweet lambs.

Cream of Tomato Soup

Connie Bryant
Topeka, KS

Grilled cheese sandwiches are a must with this creamy soup.

2 T. unsalted butter
1 onion, coarsely chopped
1 clove garlic, minced
2 T. fresh tarragon leaves,
   chopped
1/2 t. allspice
1/2 t. sugar
6 c. chicken broth

3 lbs. plum tomatoes, peeled and
   coarsely chopped
1 T. tomato paste
1 T. orange zest
1 c. whipping cream
Garnish: 2 T. fresh chives,
   snipped

Melt the butter in a large heavy pot over medium-low heat. Add onion and cook about 10 minutes or until softened. Add garlic, tarragon, allspice and sugar; cook, stirring for one minute. Add chicken broth, tomatoes and tomato paste to the pot; bring to a boil. Reduce heat to medium, partially cover and simmer for 30 minutes. Stir in orange zest and allow to cool to room temperature. Purée the soup, in batches, in a blender or food processor. Return to the pot, stir in the cream and heat through over low heat. Do not boil. Garnish with chives and serve. Makes 6 to 8 servings.

Comfort is...
Sleeping on cotton sheets that have been dried on the clothesline.

Italian Vegetable Soup

Karen Pilcher
Burleson, TX

*One of my family's all-time favorites! Not only does
it taste great...it's ready in 30 minutes.*

1 lb. ground Italian sausage
1 onion, sliced
16-oz. can chopped tomatoes,
   undrained
15-oz. can garbanzo beans,
   drained
10-1/2 oz. can beef broth

1-1/2 c. water
2 yellow squash, sliced
   shoestring-style
1/2 t. dried basil
Garnish: grated Parmesan
   cheese

In a large saucepan, cook sausage and onion until light brown, stirring
occasionally; drain. Stir in tomatoes, beans, broth, water, squash and
basil. Heat to boiling; reduce heat. Cover and simmer until the squash
is tender, about 5 minutes. Pour soup into individual bowls and
sprinkle with Parmesan cheese. Makes 6 servings.

Comfort is...
   A warm, fluffy robe after a bubble bath.

Beefy Mushroom Soup

Vicki Hockenberry
Dysart, PA

Very tasty, thick and hearty.

1/2 lb. ground beef
1 onion, chopped
2 cloves garlic, minced
1 t. Italian seasoning
2 10-3/4 oz. cans cream of
   mushroom soup
1-1/3 c. milk
1-1/3 c. water

1 carrot, shredded
1/4 c. quick-cooking barley,
   uncooked
1/4 c. macaroni, uncooked
1/4 c. long grain rice, uncooked
8-oz. pkg. mushrooms, sliced
2 T. grated Parmesan cheese

In a skillet, brown beef, onion, garlic and Italian seasoning. Drain excess grease and set aside. In a large saucepan, combine soup, milk and water; bring to a boil. Add carrot, barley, macaroni and rice. Reduce heat and simmer for approximately 20 minutes or until barley, macaroni and rice are tender. Add beef mixture, mushrooms and cheese; simmer for approximately 5 minutes, stirring occasionally. Makes 4 servings.

Comfort is...
Laughing so hard your cheeks hurt!

Cowboy Goulash

Brendon Powers
Spearville, KS

Perfect for those autumn harvest parties.

7-1/4-oz. pkg. macaroni and
  cheese
1 lb. ground beef
1/2 c. onion, chopped

1 T. chili powder
16-oz. can diced tomatoes,
  undrained
17-oz. can corn, drained

Prepare macaroni and cheese as directed on package; set aside in a
large casserole dish. Brown beef and onion in skillet; drain fat. Stir in
chili powder. Add tomatoes; simmer for 5 minutes. Add corn and stir.
Pour ground beef mixture into macaroni and cheese; mix well. Makes
6 servings.

Comfort is...
    Taking a drive on a country road.

Best-Ever Cream of Broccoli Soup
Kristine Marumoto
Salt Lake City, UT

Serve with crusty bread for a super lunch!

1/4 c. onion, finely chopped	10-oz. pkg. frozen, chopped
4 T. butter	broccoli
4 T. all-purpose flour	1 c. half-and-half
3 c. water	1 bay leaf
3 t. chicken bouillon granules	salt and pepper to taste

Sauté onion in butter until tender; blend in flour. Add water, bouillon, broccoli, half-and-half and bay leaf. Simmer until broccoli is thawed; bring to a boil. Before serving, salt and pepper to taste; remove bay leaf. Makes 4 to 6 servings.

Comfort is...
Singing along with one of your favorite songs on the radio.

Hearty Turkey Soup

Lynda Robson
Boston, MA

A fabulous way to use all that leftover
turkey from the holidays.

2 T. oil
2 c. mushrooms, sliced
8 c. chicken broth
1/3 c. barley, uncooked
1/4 c. dried, minced onion
1 t. dried sage

1/8 t. pepper
1-1/2 c. carrot, sliced
1-1/2 c. celery, sliced
1-1/2 c. zucchini, sliced
1 c. tomato, diced
2 c. cooked turkey, chopped

Heat oil in a large saucepan, add mushrooms and sauté about
5 minutes or until tender. Stir in chicken broth, barley, onion, sage and
pepper. Bring mixture to a boil, reduce heat and simmer, covered, for
about 20 minutes or until barley is almost tender. Stir in carrot, celery,
zucchini and tomato; continue to simmer, covered, for 10 minutes.
Add turkey and cook, covered, about 15 minutes or until barley and
vegetables are tender. Serves 4 to 6.

Comfort is...
Warm towels right out of the dryer.

Cream of Carrot Soup

Loretta Head
Penacook, NH

It sounds a little different, but it's worth trying!

3 c. carrots, sliced
4-1/2 c. chicken broth
1-1/2 c. onion, chopped
4 T. fresh parsley, chopped

3 c. milk
6 T. all-purpose flour
1/2 t. salt
6 T. butter

In a large saucepan, boil carrots, broth, onion and parsley until tender. Place carrot mixture into a blender and blend well. In a skillet, place milk, flour, salt and butter; cook as though making gravy. Once mixture is thick, combine with carrot mixture. Makes 4 servings.

Old-Time Potato-Corn Chowder

Sharon Vandermark
Bloomsburg, PA

Serve with homemade rolls or bread and honey...fantastic!

1 onion, diced
2 c. celery, diced
2 T. butter
8 c. potatoes, peeled and diced
16-oz. can chicken broth
4 c. water
2 c. milk

2 c. corn
1 lb. bacon, crisply cooked and
    diced
6 eggs, hard-boiled and diced
2 T. fresh parsley, chopped
2 t. salt
1 t. pepper

In a large stockpot, sauté onion and celery in butter until soft. Add potatoes, chicken broth and water. Simmer for about 25 minutes or until potatoes are cooked; mash potatoes a little to make chowder thicker. Add milk, corn, bacon and eggs; sprinkle with parsley, salt and pepper. Cover and simmer for about 20 minutes. Makes 8 to 10 servings.

Clam Chowder

Kathleen Dolge
Silver Spring, MD

*You can substitute corn, broccoli or cauliflower for the
clams and have a whole new chowder.*

1/4 lb. bacon, diced
1 T. oil
2 carrots, minced
1 onion, minced
2 potatoes, peeled and diced
3 c. milk

.87 oz. pkg. chicken gravy mix
3 6-1/2 oz. cans chopped clams,
    one can undrained, 2 drained
salt and pepper to taste
1/8 t. nutmeg
1 T. fresh parsley, chopped

In a heavy 5 to 6-quart Dutch oven, cook bacon over medium-high
heat with oil about 5 minutes; reserve drippings. Do not cook until
crispy. Add carrots and onion to bacon; sauté about 10 minutes
over medium heat. Place potatoes, milk, gravy mix and clams into
Dutch oven; simmer until potatoes are tender. Add salt, pepper
and nutmeg; stirring occasionally. Serve with a sprinkle of parsley.
Makes 8 servings.

Comfort is...
Chips & salsa!

Grandmom's Soup

Sara Wilhelm
Martinsburg, WV

*My Grandmom Burkhart used to make this soup for us on special
occasions or if we weren't feeling well...it is very special to me.*

1 bay leaf
2 T. parsley
26-oz. can pork and beans
26-oz. can peas, drained
2 15-oz. cans corn, drained
2 onions, chopped

5 potatoes, peeled and chopped
26-oz. can tomatoes
1/2 head cabbage, chopped
1/2 lb. ham bone
water to taste

Combine all ingredients in a saucepan; heat over medium heat for
approximately 2-1/2 hours. Makes 10 servings.

Irish Stew

Lera Wren
Fairfield, TX

There is nothing better than this stew on a cold and blustery evening.

5 potatoes, peeled and chopped
1 lb. ground beef, browned
1 c. water

1/2 c. all-purpose flour
2 T. chili powder
1 t. garlic

Place potatoes and beef in a Dutch oven. Add water and bring to a
light boil. Add remaining ingredients and simmer on low for about
45 minutes. Makes 4 servings.

Comfort is...
Jammies with feet!

Creamy Ham Chowder

Marian Buckley
Fontana, CA

This is the type of chowder that warms you from head to toe!

2 17-oz. cans cream-style corn
2 14-1/2 oz. cans chicken broth
1 c. cooked ham, diced

1 c. whipping cream
Garnish: 1/2 c. fresh chives,
    minced

Blend together corn and broth in a saucepan; stir in ham. Bring mixture to a simmer over medium heat, and cook for 5 minutes. Pour in cream and heat through, but do not boil. Garnish with chives. Serves 6.

Comfort is...
Running through a sprinkler!

Chicken Gumbo Soup

Carol Hickman
Kingsport, TN

Serve this gumbo soup over a bowl of fluffy rice!

4 slices bacon, browned and
   diced
1 c. onion, chopped
1 c. green pepper, chopped
1 c. celery, chopped
1 clove garlic, minced
6 boneless, skinless chicken
   breasts, cooked and chopped

4 14-1/2 oz. cans chicken broth
2 t. salt
1/4 t. pepper
15-oz. can tomato and herb
   sauce
16-oz. bag frozen, sliced okra

In a Dutch oven, place bacon, onion, green pepper, celery and garlic; sauté for 3 minutes. Add chicken, chicken broth, salt and pepper. Simmer, covered, for 30 minutes. Add tomato sauce and okra; simmer an additional 30 minutes or until okra is tender. Makes 8 to 10 servings.

Comfort is...
Bubbles and ice cream cones on a
sunny afternoon.

Bean Soup

Stephanie Argentine
Rayland, OH

My family and I all help plant a garden each year so that
we have fresh beans for this soup.

2 1-lb. ham hocks
2 c. water

4 to 5 potatoes, peeled and
    cubed
2-1/2 c. green beans, snapped

Boil ham hocks in water for about 30 minutes. Reduce heat to medium
and remove ham hocks. Remove all meat from bone and place back in
water with potatoes. Cook for 20 minutes or until tender. Add beans
to saucepan and cook about 15 minutes or until tender. Makes 4 to
6 servings.

Comfort is...
    Spending time with dear, old friends.

Tortellini-Basil Soup

Patty Spiers
Wiggins, MS

For a different taste try using spinach, tri-color or pesto tortellini.

3 10-1/2 oz. cans chicken broth
9-oz. pkg. refrigerated cheese
   tortellini, uncooked
15-oz. can navy beans, drained
1 tomato, chopped
1/2 c. fresh basil, crushed

2 T. balsamic vinegar
1/3 c. fresh Parmesan cheese,
   grated
1 t. pepper
Garnish: fresh basil sprigs

Bring broth to a boil in large Dutch oven. Add tortellini and cook
for 6 minutes or until tender. Stir in beans and tomato. Reduce heat
and simmer for 5 minutes or until thoroughly heated. Remove from
heat; stir in basil and vinegar. Ladle soup into individual bowls;
sprinkle each serving with cheese and pepper. Garnish with basil.
Makes 4 to 6 servings.

Comfort is...
Swinging on a swing!

Chicken Noodle Soup

Natalie Holdren
Overland Park, KS

This is quick, yet homemade comfort food for our family!

2 6-oz. cans shredded chicken
2 cubes chicken bouillon
4 c. water
3-oz. pkg. creamy chicken
    ramen noodles with
    seasoning packet, divided
1 t. poultry seasoning

1 T. fresh parsley, chopped
1 c. milk
4 carrots, chopped
4 stalks celery, chopped
1 c. frozen peas
1 c. frozen corn
1/2 onion, chopped

Place chicken, bouillon and water in a 4-cup measuring cup; microwave on high for 5 minutes. Add ramen noodle seasoning packet, poultry seasoning, parsley and milk. Pour chicken mixture and vegetables into a Dutch oven; boil for 5 to 7 minutes. Break ramen noodles in half and add. Boil for an additional 3 to 4 minutes. Reduce heat and serve within 5 minutes. Makes 6 to 8 servings.

Comfort is...
    Watching your favorite old movie.

Bean & Pasta Stew

Annette Ingram
Grand Rapids, MI

Whenever I'm invited to a potluck or family gathering,
I'm always asked to bring this stew!

2 c. water
1/2 c. carrot, sliced
1 T. chili powder
2 T. tomato paste
14-1/2 oz. can stewed tomatoes,
 undrained

3 10-1/2 oz. cans chicken broth
4.9-oz. pkg. bean medley with
 pasta soup mix
2 c. spinach, torn

In a large stockpot or Dutch oven, blend together water, carrot, chili powder, tomato paste, tomatoes, chicken broth and soup mix. Bring mixture to a boil, then reduce heat. Simmer, uncovered, for 25 minutes or until beans are tender. Add spinach and cook an additional 5 minutes. Makes 4 to 6 servings.

Comfort is...
Morning sunlight shining through
a spider's web.

Easy Potato & Bacon Soup

Mindy Beard
Yorktown, IN

Very quick and easy!

1 c. water
2 c. potatoes, peeled and cubed
1/2 t. salt
1/2 t. pepper
10-3/4 oz. can cream of chicken
    soup
1-3/4 c. milk

1 c. sour cream
8 slices bacon, crisply cooked
    and chopped
1 T. fresh parsley, chopped
1 onion, finely chopped
Garnish: Cheddar cheese,
    shredded

In a 3-quart saucepan, combine water, potatoes, salt and pepper; bring to a boil. Cover and simmer, stirring frequently, for about 10 minutes or until potatoes are tender. Gradually add soup and milk, stirring constantly. Stir in sour cream, bacon, parsley and onion; heat through. Top with cheese. Makes 2 to 4 servings.

Comfort is...
A grilled cheese sandwich with tomato soup.

Comfort Soup

Jan Barry
Woodridge, IL

Add your favorite vegetables or cheese to this soup!

10-oz. pkg. frozen, chopped
   broccoli, thawed
10-1/2 oz. can cream of potato
   soup

1 c. milk
1 c. mild Cheddar cheese,
   shredded

In a large microwave-safe dish, heat broccoli. Add soup, milk and cheese; stir. Heat in microwave until hot and the cheese is melted. Makes 3 to 4 servings.

Mushroom & Chive Soup

Dorothy Schrock
Millersburg, OH

Serve with flat bread for a satisfying supper!

1/2 c. butter
2 c. fresh mushrooms, finely
   chopped
1/4 c. all-purpose flour
1/4 t. dry mustard

1/2 t. salt
2 c. chicken broth
2 c. half-and-half
1/4 c. chives, finely chopped

Melt butter in saucepan. Add mushrooms and sauté until tender. Stir in flour, mustard and salt. Cook, stirring constantly, for one minute. Pour in chicken broth and cook, stirring constantly until thickened. Stir in half-and-half and chives. Heat thoroughly, but do not boil. Makes 4 to 6 servings.

Comfort is...
   A warm bowl of oatmeal for breakfast.

Fresh Tomato Soup

April Jacobs
Loveland, CO

*This is a nice change from traditional tomato
soup. It's perfect for a light lunch!*

2 c. carrots, sliced
1 c. celery, chopped
1 onion, finely chopped
1/2 c. green pepper, chopped
1/4 c. butter
4-1/2 c. chicken broth, divided

4 tomatoes, peeled and chopped
4 t. sugar
1/2 t. curry powder
1/2 t. salt
1/4 t. pepper
1/4 c. all-purpose flour

In a Dutch oven, sauté carrots, celery, onion and green pepper in
butter until tender. Add 4 cups broth, tomatoes, sugar, curry powder,
salt and pepper; bring to a boil. Reduce heat; simmer for 20 minutes.
In a small bowl, combine the flour and remaining broth until smooth.
Gradually add to soup. Bring to a boil; cook and stir for 2 minutes.
Makes 9 servings.

Comfort is...
A surprise bouquet of flowers.

Winter Bean Soup

Kay Marone
Des Moines, IA

You need to start this the night before...but it's worth it!

1/2 lb. dried Great Northern
   beans
1/2 lb. dried red kidney beans
1/2 lb. dried pinto beans
2 T. butter
1 c. celery, chopped
1 onion, diced

1-1/2 lb. ham hock
1 bay leaf
1 t. peppercorns
7 c. water
1 lb. smoked sausage, sliced
salt to taste

Cover beans with water and soak overnight. Drain, rinse and set aside.
In a 4-quart soup kettle, melt butter and sauté celery and onion for
5 minutes. Add ham hock, bay leaf, peppercorns, beans and water;
cover and simmer for one hour. Add sausage, cover and simmer for an
additional 20 minutes. Remove ham hock and bay leaf. Salt to taste.
Makes 6 servings.

Comfort is...
Reading in bed and eating a bowl of
macaroni & cheese.

Nothing Soothes the Soul Like Homemade Soup

Cauliflower-Cheese Soup

Terri Dillingham
Windsor, NY

This is my entire family's favorite wintertime dish...served with some homemade muffins, it warms the tummy.

1 cauliflower head, chopped
1 c. celery, diced
1 c. onion, diced
6-1/2 c. water, divided
8-oz. pkg. cream cheese

1/2 c. cornstarch
2 lbs. Cheddar cheese, grated
2 c. milk
1 t. parsley
salt and pepper to taste

In large saucepan, simmer vegetables in 6 cups water until tender; drain. Add cream cheese. In a small bowl, dissolve cornstarch in remaining water, then add to saucepan. Blend in Cheddar cheese. Add milk, parsley, salt and pepper. Heat until ready to serve. Makes 6 to 8 servings.

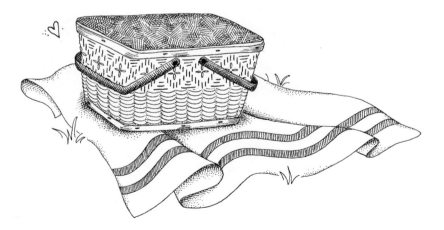

Comfort is...
Watching a hot air balloon
floating in the sky.

Sour Cream & Wild Rice Soup

Cheri Maxwell
Gulf Breeze, FL

*My father's mother always made this for my dad...I found the recipe
when I was looking through my parents' wedding album.*

4 slices bacon, chopped
1/2 c. onion, chopped
1 c. celery, chopped
1/3 c. all-purpose flour
1/8 t. pepper

14-1/2 oz. can chicken broth
1-3/4 c. wild rice, cooked
1 c. sour cream
2 c. milk

In a 2-quart saucepan, cook bacon over medium-high heat until
bacon begins to brown, about 3 to 5 minutes. Add onion and celery;
continue cooking, stirring occasionally, until bacon is brown and
vegetables are crisp-tender, about 5 to 7 minutes. Reduce heat to
medium; stir in flour and pepper. With wire whisk, stir in broth.
Cook over medium heat for 3 to 4 minutes, stirring constantly, or
until mixture thickens and comes to a full boil. Boil one minute,
stirring constantly. Stir in wild rice, sour cream and milk. Continue
cooking until heated through, 4 to 6 minutes. Makes 6 servings.

Comfort is...
Visiting the hometown where you grew up.

Herbed Vegetable Soup

Robbin Chamberlain
Worthington, OH

This makes a lot of soup....freeze and reheat
when you need a pick-me-up.

1/4 c. olive oil
1/4 c. garlic, minced
1 c. onion, diced
1 c. celery, sliced
1 c. carrots, sliced
1 T. fresh basil, chopped
1 T. fresh thyme, chopped
1 T. fresh oregano, chopped

1/8 t. cayenne pepper
2 14-1/2-oz. cans crushed
  tomatoes, undrained
4 to 6 c. water
1 c. zucchini, chopped
1 c. yellow squash, chopped
salt and pepper to taste
3 T. sugar

Heat oil in large stockpot; add garlic, onion, celery and carrots. Cover and cook on low heat until carrots are tender. Add basil, thyme, oregano, cayenne pepper and tomatoes. Thin with water to desired consistency. Simmer for 1/2 hour. Add zucchini and squash. Simmer an additional 1/2 hour. Season with salt and pepper. Add sugar and stir. Makes 8 to 10 servings.

Comfort is...
Tossing a penny in a fountain,
and making a wish.

Hearty Chicken & Dumpling Soup

Kara Allison
Dublin, OH

This is the quickest and tastiest dumpling soup recipe!

16-oz. can chicken broth
10-3/4 oz. can cream of chicken
   soup
10-3/4 oz. can cream of
   mushroom soup
10-3/4 oz. can chicken and
   dumplings
1 c. celery, chopped

1 c. sweet onion, chopped
1 c. carrot, sliced
1 c. potatoes, chopped
1 c. peas
1 c. corn
1 bay leaf
salt and pepper to taste

Combine all ingredients in a large soup pot and simmer over low heat for 2 hours. Remove bay leaf and serve. Makes 4 servings.

Comfort is...
      Building a sandcastle.

Don't Watch Me Minestrone

Denise Rounds
Tulsa, OK

Some days are so hectic that I need a meal I can start before I leave home. This soup is perfect...there's nothing like coming home to a kitchen that smells like dinner is ready.

1 lb. stew meat, cubed	2 c. cabbage, finely sliced
6 c. water	1 zucchini, thinly sliced
28-oz. can chopped tomatoes, undrained	16-oz. can garbanzo beans, drained
2 cubes beef bouillon	1 c. elbow macaroni, uncooked
1 onion, chopped	1/4 c. grated Parmesan cheese
2 T. dried vegetable flakes	

In a slow cooker, combine meat, water, tomatoes, bouillon, onion, vegetable flakes and cabbage. Cover and cook on low for 7 to 9 hours or until the meat is tender. Add zucchini, beans and macaroni. Cook on high for 30 to 40 minutes or until vegetables are tender. Serve with Parmesan sprinkled over individual servings. Makes 8 servings.

Comfort is...
Sitting in a window seat and gazing at the stars.

Vegetable Medley Stew

Cory Braun
Oak Creek, WI

Perfect after an afternoon of raking leaves!

3 boneless, skinless chicken
   breasts
1 onion, coarsely chopped
2 c. water
2 15-oz. cans stewed tomatoes
2 to 3 carrots, sliced
1 green pepper, coarsely chopped

2 potatoes, diced
1/2 t. pepper
1 t. rosemary
1 t. Italian seasonings
4 cloves garlic, crushed
4 c. rice, cooked

In a large stockpot, simmer chicken and onion in water for
25 minutes, or until juices run clear when chicken is pierced. Remove
chicken from stockpot and set aside. To broth, add tomatoes, carrots,
green pepper, potatoes, pepper, rosemary, Italian seasoning and garlic.
Simmer vegetables while cutting chicken breasts into bite-size pieces;
add to stew. Continue to cook on low for an additional 30 minutes
or until carrots and potatoes are tender. Add rice and let simmer
10 minutes longer. Makes 8 servings.

Comfort is...
   Waking up without an alarm clock.

Farmstyle Beef Stew

Carol Brashear
Myerstown, PA

*I found this recipe while looking through a cupboard at my dad's
house...it was even written in my late grandmother's handwriting!*

2 T. shortening	1 T. salt
3 lbs. stew meat, cubed	pepper to taste
2 onions, sliced	3-1/4 c. water, divided
2 cloves garlic, minced	1 c. peas
1 c. celery, chopped	12 carrots, sliced
1/4 c. fresh parsley, chopped	12 onions, chopped
2-1/2 c. canned tomatoes	6 potatoes, cubed
1/2 t. dried thyme	1/2 c. all-purpose flour

Melt shortening in a large saucepan and brown meat. Add sliced
onions, garlic, celery, parsley, tomatoes, thyme, salt, pepper and
2-1/2 cups water. Bring to a boil, reduce heat and cover; simmer for
2 hours. Add remaining vegetables and simmer for one hour. Blend
flour with remaining water and stir into stew; simmer for 5 minutes.
Makes 6 servings.

Comfort is...
Smelling lilacs in bloom.

Potato-Sausage Soup

Grace Woodruff
Pine Bluff, AR

This soup is good with a simple pan of cornbread and nothing more. It is one of our all-time favorites!

1 lb. ground sausage
1 onion, chopped
32-oz. can chicken broth
4 c. frozen, shredded hash browns
10-3/4 oz. can cream of celery soup
10-3/4 oz. can cream of chicken soup
12-oz. can evaporated milk
Garnish: Cheddar cheese, shredded

Brown sausage and onion in Dutch oven over medium heat, stirring until the sausage crumbles and is no longer pink and the onion is translucent; drain and return to Dutch oven. Add chicken broth and hash browns; bring to a boil. Cover and reduce heat; simmer for 30 minutes. In a separate saucepan, heat soups until they are blended and creamy; add milk and set aside. After sausage mixture is done simmering, add soup mixture; stir often until thoroughly blended and heated through. Sprinkle each serving with cheese. Makes 6 to 8 servings.

Comfort is...
Watching a stranger help another stranger.

Pasta Fagioli

Christine Moutinho
Acushnet, MA

Serve with some yummy rolls for dipping!

1/2 lb. ground pork
1 onion, finely chopped
1/2 clove garlic, minced
2 14-oz. cans chicken broth
14-oz. can Italian-style chopped
   tomatoes, undrained
15-oz. can red beans, drained

1 T. fresh oregano, chopped
1/4 t. cayenne pepper
1/2 t. salt
1/2 t. pepper
1/4 c. barley, uncooked
1/2 to 1 c. macaroni shells,
   uncooked

In a large saucepan, crumble and brown pork. Stir in onion and garlic; cook about 3 minutes or until onion is soft. Stir in remaining ingredients; bring to a boil and reduce heat. Simmer for 12 minutes or until pasta is tender. Makes 6 servings.

Comfort is...
pink lemonade in the summertime.

Suzi's Gumbo

Suzi Schweer
Tripoli, IA

We are a farm family from Iowa and don't usually eat spicy dishes...but this is one of our favorites.

2 c. beef broth
14-oz. can tomatoes, undrained
1 t. sugar
1/2 t. dried thyme
1/2 t. chili powder
1/4 t. pepper
1/2 t. cayenne pepper
1 to 2 T. olive oil
4 cloves garlic, chopped

1 onion, coarsely chopped
1/2 c. celery, chopped
1 green pepper, coarsely chopped
2/3 lb. shrimp, peeled and
   deveined
2 boneless, skinless chicken
   breasts, poached and cubed
3 c. white rice, cooked

In a medium saucepan, combine broth, tomatoes, sugar, thyme, chili powder, pepper and cayenne pepper; simmer for 10 minutes. In a non-stick pan, heat olive oil. Add garlic, onion and celery; sauté for 4 to 5 minutes or until onion is crisp-tender. Add green pepper and cook for 2 to 3 minutes. Add onion mixture to the saucepan and simmer for 10 minutes. Add shrimp, chicken and rice. Makes 12 servings.

Comfort is...
pizza with extra cheese!

Stuffed Pepper Soup

Christa Kerr
DuBois, PA

This soup is fabulous served with warm, crusty bread and butter.

1-1/2 lbs. ground beef
salt to taste
1-1/2 t. Worcestershire sauce
1 onion, coarsely chopped
3 green peppers, diced
3 28-oz. cans tomato sauce

1/4 t. celery seed
1/4 t. nutmeg
1/4 t. marjoram
1/3 c. brown sugar, packed
1-1/2 c. rice, uncooked

Brown ground beef with salt and Worcestershire sauce in a large soup pot. Add next 7 ingredients and three, 28-ounce cans of water. Bring to a slow boil, then lower heat and simmer gently for 1/2 hour or until peppers are tender. Add rice and continue to simmer for 45 minutes to one hour, or until rice is cooked. Makes 10 to 12 servings.

Comfort is...
Teaching a child to ride a bike.

Lazy Day Stew

Kimberly Rockett
Twin Falls, ID

Super-simple, but full of taste...and it makes the house smell wonderful!

2 lbs. round steak, cubed
4 potatoes, coarsely chopped
6 carrots, coarsely chopped
5 onions, coarsely chopped
3 stalks celery, coarsely chopped
15-oz. can tomato sauce
1 c. water
2 t. sugar
salt and pepper to taste
4 t. quick-cooking tapioca mix, uncooked

Arrange steak in a 3-quart casserole dish. Layer vegetables on top of steak. In a medium bowl, mix together tomato sauce, water and sugar. Pour over meat and vegetables. Salt and pepper to taste. Scatter tapioca on top; do not stir in. Place a piece of aluminum foil over top and cover with a lid. Bake at 325 degrees for 2 to 3 hours. Do not open during cooking time. Makes 4 to 6 servings.

Comfort is...
Slices of freshly-baked bread with melted butter.

Chilly Day Chili

Judy Bovich
Little Canada, MN

Serve with rice and some grated Cheddar cheese...yum!

1-1/2 lbs. ground turkey
1 onion, chopped
1 green pepper, chopped
3 cloves garlic, crushed
2 T. chili powder
2 T. cumin
1 t. dried oregano

1 t. dried basil
salt and pepper to taste
28-oz. can crushed tomatoes, undrained
15-1/2 oz. can pinto beans, drained
1/2 T. Dijon mustard

In a saucepan, cook turkey, onion, green pepper and garlic. Stir in chili powder, cumin, oregano, basil, salt and pepper. Add tomatoes; cook for 20 to 30 minutes. Mix in beans and Dijon mustard; cook for an additional 30 minutes. Makes 4 to 6 servings.

Comfort is...
Fireworks in the evening sky.

Dad's Western Soup

Pam Ludwig
Imboden, AR

Fresh-from-the-oven cornbread is sensational with this soup!

2 lbs. ground beef, browned
2 10-oz. cans tomatoes with
   chilies, undrained
8-oz. can tomato sauce
16-oz. can diced tomatoes,
   undrained

15-oz. can ranch-style beans,
   drained
15-oz. can corn, drained
1-1/4 oz. pkg. taco seasoning
1-oz. pkg. dry ranch dressing
   mix

In a large saucepan, combine beef, tomatoes with chilies, tomato sauce, tomatoes, beans and corn; mix well. Add taco seasoning and dressing mix. Simmer for 30 minutes. Makes 6 servings.

Comfort is...
Reading in bed.

Chicken Jambalaya

Lynn Williams
Muncie, IN

*My sister-in-law from Louisiana shared this
recipe with me...it is fabulous!*

8 c. chicken broth
3-lb. chicken
2 lbs. smoked sausage, sliced
1/2 lb. ham, diced
4 c. onion, chopped
1/2 c. celery, chopped
2 T. soy sauce
1 c. green onions, chopped

1 T. garlic, minced
1 c. green pepper, finely chopped
1/2 t. cayenne pepper
2 bay leaves
1/2 t. dried thyme
1/2 t. dried sage
2 c. long-grain rice, uncooked
salt and pepper to taste

Add broth and chicken to a stockpot, bring to a boil, then reduce
to simmer. Cook, uncovered, for 45 minutes, or until juices run clear
when chicken is pierced. Remove chicken from broth; reserving broth
in stockpot. When chicken is cool enough to handle, remove meat and
cube; set aside. Place sausage and ham in a Dutch oven; cook over
medium heat until lightly brown. Set aside sausage and ham, leaving
drippings in Dutch oven. Add onion and celery to Dutch oven and
sauté over medium heat about 30 minutes. Blend in soy sauce and
cook for one additional minute. Add green onions, garlic and green
pepper; cook 5 minutes longer. Stir in cayenne, bay leaves, thyme and
sage, 3 cups reserved broth and bring to a boil. Blend in rice, reduce
heat to a simmer and cook, covered, for 20 minutes. Stir in chicken,
sausage and ham and continue to cook until all liquid is absorbed and
rice is tender, about 10 minutes. Remove bay leaves. Add salt and
pepper to taste. Makes 8 servings.

Comfort is...
grandma's fluffy biscuits.

Potato & Vegetable Stew

Connie Hilty
Pearland, TX

My children and I love to prepare this stew together...it's not only tasty but fun to make!

2 c. chicken broth	15-1/4 oz. can corn, drained
1 potato, diced	15-1/4 oz. can lima beans,
1/4 onion, chopped	drained
14-1/2 oz. can tomatoes,	1/2 t. pepper
drained	1/4 c. instant mashed potatoes

In a large pot, heat chicken broth over medium heat to boiling. Add potato; bring back to boil and cook for 5 minutes. Add onion, tomatoes, corn, lima beans and pepper. Bring to a low boil. Cover and cook for 20 minutes. Stir in instant potatoes until mixed. Makes 6 to 8 servings.

for a special friend

Comfort is...
When a friend says, "You're someone special."

Italian Wedding Soup

Darrell Lawry
Kissimmee, FL

*This soup was served at my daughter's wedding...I had to beg
the caterer to share the recipe with me!*

1/2 lb. ground beef
1 egg, beaten
2 T. bread crumbs
1 T. grated Parmesan cheese
1/2 t. dried basil
1/2 t. onion powder

5-3/4 c. chicken broth
2 c. escarole, thinly sliced
1/2 c. orzo, uncooked
1/3 c. carrot, finely chopped
Garnish: Parmesan cheese,
   grated

Combine beef, egg, bread crumbs, cheese, basil and onion powder;
shape into 3/4-inch balls. Heat broth to boiling; stir in escarole, orzo,
carrot and meatballs; return to boil and reduce heat to medium.
Cook at slow boil for 10 minutes or until orzo is tender to bite. Stir
frequently to prevent sticking. Serve with Parmesan cheese on top.
Makes 4 to 6 servings.

Comfort is...
Kissing your dog on the head.

White Chili

Kathy Grashoff
Ft. Wayne, IN

Garnish with yellow or blue corn chips for a festive look.

2 T. oil
1 onion, finely chopped
4-oz. can chopped, green chilies
2 t. garlic powder
2 t. salt
2 t. cumin
2 t. dried oregano

2 t. coriander
1/2 t. cayenne pepper
2 15.8-oz. can Great Northern
  beans, undrained
2 10-1/2 oz. cans chicken broth
2 5-oz. cans chicken, drained

In a large stockpot, heat oil over medium heat. Add onion; sauté until brown. Add green chilies, garlic powder, salt, cumin, oregano, coriander and cayenne pepper; stir until well blended. Add remaining ingredients; bring to a boil. Reduce heat to low. Simmer for 15 to 20 minutes or until heated through. Makes 8 to 10 servings.

Comfort is...
Watching an older couple hold hands.

Chicken Tortellini Soup

Mary Bettuchy
Duxbury, MA

A great year 'round recipe...it is just packed
full of "good for you" ingredients!

8 c. chicken broth
1 c. carrots, diced
1 c. celery, chopped
1 onion, diced
2 bay leaves
1 t. dried thyme

2 T. dried parsley
1 t. pepper
1-1/2 c. boneless, skinless
    chicken breasts, cooked and
    diced
1 c. cheese tortellini

Over low heat, simmer chicken broth, carrots, celery, onion, bay
leaves, thyme, parsley and pepper about one hour or until vegetables
are tender. Bring to a gentle boil; add chicken and tortellini; boil about
5 to 10 minutes, or until tortellini rises to the surface. Remove bay
leaves. Makes 8 servings.

Comfort is...
A steaming bowl of chili with crackers.

Sausage-Bean Soup

Betty Kokal
St. Louis, MO

Serve with Italian bread drizzled with garlic sauce!

3/4 lb. ground Italian sausage
1/2 c. onion, chopped
1 clove garlic, minced
15-1/2 oz. can baby butter
  beans, rinsed and drained
15-oz. can black beans, rinsed
  and drained

14-1/2 oz. can diced tomatoes,
  undrained
14-1/2 oz. can beef broth
1 T. fresh basil, minced
1 T. grated Parmesan cheese

In a large saucepan, cook sausage, onion and garlic until sausage is browned; drain. Add beans, tomatoes, broth and basil. Cover and simmer for 10 minutes. Sprinkle each serving with Parmesan cheese. Makes 4 to 6 servings.

Comfort is...
  The smell of freshly-popped popcorn!

Cream of Pumpkin Soup

Janice Gilmer
Merrimack, NH

Make your own crusty bread and serve a big
Caesar salad with this soup...tasty!

2 T. butter
1 onion, diced
29-oz. can pumpkin
1 bay leaf
2 carrots, chopped

3 13-3/4 oz. cans chicken broth
1 T. brown sugar packed
1 c. light cream
1/2 t. nutmeg

In a large saucepan, melt butter and sauté onion. Add pumpkin, bay leaf, carrots, broth and brown sugar. Bring to a boil, reduce heat and simmer for 15 minutes. Purée mixture in blender and return to pan; stir in cream and nutmeg. Makes 8 servings.

Comfort is...
an icy root beer float!

Golden Summer Soup

Stephanie Mayer
Portsmouth, VA

An absolutely beautiful and delicious soup.

1 onion, chopped	3 c. chicken broth
2 T. oil	1 c. buttermilk
2 to 3 Roma tomatoes, chopped	1/4 c. fresh basil, minced
1-1/2 lbs. yellow squash, chopped	Garnish: Roma tomatoes, sliced and fresh basil

In a large pan, sauté onion in oil over medium heat about 10 minutes or until golden. Add tomatoes and stir for about 5 minutes or until soft. Add squash and broth to pan. Bring to a boil over high heat. Cover and simmer for about 15 to 20 minutes, or until squash is tender. Purée mixture with buttermilk in a blender or food processor until smooth. Stir in basil. Serve warm or cold, garnish with basil and thin round slices of Roma tomato floating on top. Makes 6 to 8 servings.

Comfort is...
A dream that comes true.

Squash & Wild Rice Soup

Kathy Grashoff
Ft. Wayne, IN

Colorful and full of flavor!

1/4 c. butter	4 c. yellow squash, sliced
1 c. onion, finely chopped	1/2 c. carrot, shredded
1/2 c. celery, finely chopped	1/2 c. white rice, uncooked
3 cloves garlic, minced	3/4 t. salt
5 14-1/2 oz. cans chicken broth	1/2 t. pepper
1/2 c. wild rice, uncooked	3/4 t. dried basil
4 c. zucchini, sliced	1/2 t. dried oregano

In a large Dutch oven, melt butter over medium heat. Add onion, celery and garlic. Cook about 3 minutes or until vegetables are tender, stirring frequently. Add chicken broth and wild rice; bring mixture to a boil. Reduce heat to medium low. Cover and cook an additional 30 minutes. Stir in zucchini, squash, carrot, rice, salt and pepper. Increase heat to high and bring mixture back to a boil. Reduce heat to low. Cover and simmer for 20 minutes or until rice is tender. Stir in basil and oregano. Makes 10 to 12 servings.

Comfort is...
Making s'mores over the campfire on a chilly autumn night.

Cheese Soup

Pat Burson
Brewster, OH

Simple, quick and tasty!

1/2 c. all-purpose flour
1 stick butter
1 qt. milk
1/2 lb. pasteurized process
   cheese spread, cubed

1/2 t. onion, finely chopped
1/2 t. seasoned salt
15-oz. can mixed vegetables,
   drained
Garnish: seasoned croutons

In saucepan, over medium heat, make a paste with flour and butter. Slowly add milk; stir. Add remaining ingredients; blend until cheese melts and becomes thick. Serve with croutons on top. Makes 4 to 6 servings.

Comfort is...
   Finding a fantastic bargain at a yard sale!

Creamy Clam Bisque

Pamela Jaeger
Farmington, MI

*A welcome addition to a cool, autumn evening! I really
appreciate the ease with which it's made in
such a short amount of time!*

10-3/4 oz. can cream of chicken
  soup
10-3/4 oz. can cream of celery
  soup
1-1/3 c. half-and-half

2 6-1/2 oz. cans minced clams,
  undrained
1/4 t. cayenne pepper
1/4 c. dry vermouth
Garnish: butter, paprika and
  green onion tops

In a large saucepan, stir together soups and half-and-half. Cook over
medium-low heat, stirring occasionally, until the mixture simmers.
Add clams and cayenne pepper; heat through, but do not boil. Stir in
vermouth; heat through. Garnish each serving with a pat of butter, a
dash of paprika and onion tops. Makes 8 servings.

Comfort is...
*Cuddling with your favorite
stuffed animal.*

Three Onion Soup

Tim Macklin
Hoffman Estates, IL

*A delicious and fresh tasting soup compared
to traditional onion soup.*

1 t. olive oil
2 c. leeks, chopped
1 onion, thinly sliced
2 shallots, thinly sliced
salt and pepper to taste
1-1/2 c. water, divided

1 potato, peeled and cubed
1 c. chicken broth
Garnish: 1/2 c. Gruyère cheese,
   grated and 2 t. balsamic
   vinegar

Heat oil in a 10" non-stick skillet over medium heat until hot. Place leeks, onion, shallots, salt and pepper into skillet. Cook, stirring occasionally, for 15 minutes or until vegetable edges are golden brown. Add 1/2 cup water to skillet and use a rubber spatula to loosen any remaining glaze. Transfer mixture to a saucepan. Add potato, broth and remaining water to onion mixture. Simmer, covered, stirring occasionally, until potatoes are tender. Purée one cup of mixture in blender and stir into remaining soup. Season with salt and pepper. Serve soup sprinkled with cheese and drizzled with vinegar. Makes 4 servings.

Comfort is...
Watching the sunrise from your flower garden.

Taco Soup

Susan Nafziger
Canton, KS

Serve with lime-flavored corn chips...yummy!

1-1/2 lbs. ground beef, browned
   and drained
1 onion, chopped
1-oz. pkg. taco seasoning
1-oz. pkg. dry ranch salad
   dressing mix
water to taste
16-oz. pkg. frozen corn

15-oz. can kidney beans,
   undrained
15-oz. can tomato sauce
15-oz. can tomatoes with green
   chilies, undrained
Garnish: corn chips, Cheddar
   cheese, shredded and sour
   cream

In a soup pot, simmer all ingredients together for 20 to 30 minutes. To serve, top with corn chips, grated cheese and sour cream. Makes 6 to 8 servings.

Comfort is...
Noticing that the new birdhouse you put up has occupants!

Homebaked Breads & Rolls

Yeast

WHEN buttermilk
& Honey & Flour
rise to the occasion
to create
Homemade breads
& rolls...

Warm from the oven

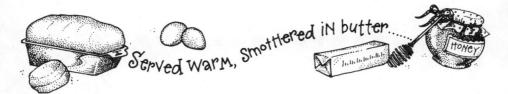

Served warm, smothered in butter....

Yummy Honey Cornbread

Anita Benoit
Manchester, ME

Be sure not to overmix! It's the key to good cornbread.

1 c. all-purpose flour
1 T. baking powder
1/2 t. salt
3/4 c. cornmeal
1/4 c. sugar

1 c. whipping cream
1/4 c. oil
1/3 c. honey
2 eggs, beaten

In a large mixing bowl, sift together flour, baking powder and salt. Add cornmeal. In a separate bowl, stir remaining ingredients together and add to flour mixture; do not overmix. Place into a greased 9"x9" baking pan. Bake at 400 degrees for 20 minutes. Makes 10 to 12 servings.

Honey Butter:

1 c. butter

1/4 c. honey

Whip butter and honey together until smooth, then serve over warm cornbread.

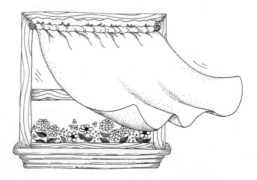

Comfort is...
Opening all the windows and feeling the breeze
blow through the house.

Flint Hills Biscuits

Pat Habiger
Spearville, KS

Whole-wheat flour makes these biscuits so hearty!

1-1/2 c. all-purpose flour
1/2 c. whole-wheat flour
2 T. sugar
1 T. baking powder
1/2 t. cream of tartar

1/2 t. salt
1/2 c. shortening
1 egg
1/2 c. milk

In a medium mixing bowl, stir together flour, whole-wheat flour, sugar, baking powder, cream of tartar and salt. Cut the shortening into the dry ingredients until the mixture resembles coarse crumbs. Make a well in the center. Combine egg and milk; add all at once to flour mixture. Stir mixture until dough just clings together. On a lightly floured surface, knead gently 10 to 12 strokes, roll or pat to 1/2-inch thickness. Cut with 2-1/2 inch biscuit cutter, dipping cutter in flour between cuts; transfer to a greased baking sheet. Bake at 375 degrees for 15 to 18 minutes or until golden brown. Serve warm. Makes about 10 biscuits.

Comfort is...
a field of sunflowers.

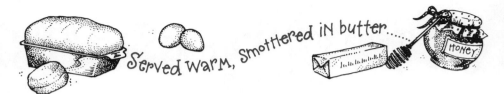

Pineapple-Zucchini Bread

Joyce Wilson
Lonaconing, MD

Serve with a tasty fruit salad for a terrific brunch.

3 eggs
1 c. oil
2 c. sugar
2 t. vanilla extract
2 t. baking soda
1 t. salt
1/4 t. baking powder
1-1/2 t. cinnamon

2 c. zucchini, shredded
3/4 t. nutmeg
8-oz. can crushed pineapple,
   drained
1 c. raisins
3 c. all-purpose flour
1 c. chopped walnuts

In a mixing bowl, beat eggs, oil, sugar and vanilla until thick. Stir in remaining ingredients; blend well. Pour into 2 greased and floured 9"x5" loaf pans. Bake at 350 degrees for one hour. Makes 2 loaves.

Comfort is...
Sitting on the front porch in a rocking chair.

Maple Nut Twist

Gay Snyder
Deerfield, OH

Every year, I make a special plate of these for the neighbors. I had to skip a year due to a birth in my family, and they sure let me know how much they missed them!

1/2 c. milk
1/4 c. margarine
1 pkg. active dry yeast
1/4 c. warm water
1/3 c. plus 3 T. sugar, divided
1-1/2 t. salt
2 eggs, beaten
3-1/4 to 3-1/2 c. plus 2 T.
   all-purpose flour, divided

1/2 c. brown sugar, packed
1/2 c. chopped walnuts
1/4 c. maple syrup
1/4 c. margarine, softened
1/2 t. cinnamon
1/2 t. maple extract
1 c. powdered sugar
1 to 2 T. water

In saucepan, heat milk and margarine until margarine is melted. In a large bowl, dissolve yeast in warm water; add 3 tablespoons sugar, salt, eggs and 2 cups flour; beat until smooth. Blend in milk and margarine mixture. Add 1-1/4 to 1-1/2 cups flour; knead until smooth. Let rise in a covered bowl. In a medium bowl, combine brown sugar, walnuts, remaining sugar, maple syrup, softened margarine, remaining flour and cinnamon; set aside. Punch dough down and divide in half; roll each half into a 14"x8" rectangle. Spread filling over each rectangle. Starting with 14-inch edge, roll up jelly roll-style. With a sharp knife, cut down the center of the jelly roll lengthwise; twist 2 pieces together to form a rope braid. Turn ends under, shape into a ring. Place dough into a greased 9" pie pan and let rise. Bake at 350 degrees for 25 minutes or until golden brown. Mix together remaining ingredients; glaze while warm. Makes 16 to 20 servings.

Comfort is...
A warm hug from Mom after your first day at school.

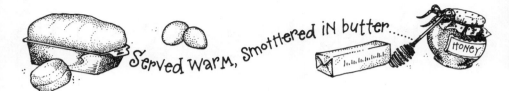

Served warm, smottered in butter......

Lemon Fans

Cindy Watson
Gooseberry Patch

*For a little variety...try using orange zest
instead of lemon zest!*

2 pkgs. active dry yeast
1/4 c. warm water
1 c. milk
2 eggs
1/3 c. sugar

2 t. lemon zest
1-1/2 t. salt
4 to 4-1/2 c. all-purpose flour
1/4 c. butter, melted and divided

In a large bowl, dissolve yeast in water. Let stand about 5 to 10 minutes or until foamy. In a small bowl, mix together milk and eggs. Stir milk mixture, sugar, lemon zest and salt into yeast mixture. Using a heavy-duty electric mixer fitted with a paddle attachment and set on low speed, beat in flour, 1/2 cup at a time, until a dough forms. On a floured surface, knead dough until smooth and elastic, about 5 to 10 minutes, adding more flour to prevent sticking. Place dough in a large greased bowl, turning to coat. Cover loosely with a damp cloth; let rise in a warm place until doubled, about one hour. Divide dough in half. On a floured surface, using a floured rolling pin, roll each dough half into an 1/8-inch thick rectangle. Brush with 1/8 cup butter. Cut each rectangle crosswise into 1-1/2 inch wide strips. Stack 6 strips on top of each other. Cut each stack crosswise into twelve, 1-1/2 inch squares. To prepare rolls, place 6 dough squares, cut side down, in each greased muffin pan cup. Brush tops with remaining butter. Cover, again; let rise in a warm place until almost doubled, about 20 minutes. Bake at 400 degrees for 10 to 15 minutes, or until golden. Transfer pans to wire racks to cool slightly. Turn rolls out onto racks to cool completely. Makes 24 rolls.

Quick Jam Biscuits

Kathy Grashoff
Ft. Wayne, IN

Use your family's favorite jam to make these biscuits extra special!

2 c. plus 2 T. biscuit baking mix, divided
6 T. buttermilk

6 T. milk
6 t. your favorite jam

In a medium bowl, stir 2 cups biscuit baking mix with buttermilk and milk until soft dough forms. If dough is too sticky, gradually add in enough of the remaining baking mix, up to 2 tablespoons to make dough easier to handle. Turn dough onto a floured surface. Knead dough about 10 times, then roll dough to 1/4-inch thickness. Cut the dough with a 2 to 3-inch cutter. Cut out the centers of half the cut biscuits using the plastic top from a 2-liter bottle. Spread uncut biscuits onto a greased baking sheet; top with biscuits with the centers cut out. Fill holes with about one teaspoon of jam per biscuit. Bake at 450 degrees for about 9 minutes or until golden. Makes 6 biscuits.

Comfort is...
Laying in the grass and looking up to find shapes in the clouds.

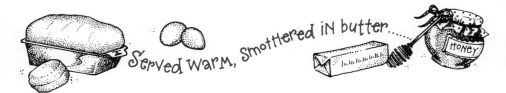

Served warm, smothered in butter...

Kitchen Oatmeal Bread

Judy Borecky
Escondido, CA

Take this bread to your next bake sale...it's sure to be a hit!

3 pkgs. active dry yeast
2-1/2 c. warm water, divided
2 c. quick-cooking oats,
   uncooked
1-3/4 c. brown sugar, packed
3/4 c. oil

1/4 c. molasses
2 c. boiling water
1/2 c. wheat germ
2 t. salt
2 c. whole-wheat flour
10 c. all-purpose flour

Dissolve yeast in 1/2 cup warm water; set aside. In a large bowl, stir together oats, brown sugar, oil and molasses. Add boiling water; let cool to lukewarm. Stir in remaining warm water; blend. Add remaining ingredients and yeast mixture; mix well. Knead until smooth and elastic. Place in a large, oiled bowl. Cover and let rise until double. Punch down and shape into 3 loaves. Place into 3 lightly greased 9"x5" loaf pans and let rise until light. Bake at 375 degrees for 45 minutes or until done. Remove from pans and let cool on wire racks. Makes 3 loaves.

Comfort is...
Finding charming old books in a shop and squirreling them home.

Monkey Bread

*Janet Schrot
Kinnelon, NJ*

On Christmas morning we sit around the tree with our coffee and hot cocoa and nibble on this great treat while we open presents!

2 10-oz. tubes refrigerated
    biscuits
1/2 c. plus 1/3 c. sugar, divided

1/2 t. cinnamon
1-1/2 sticks butter

Cut each biscuit into 4 pieces. In a plastic bag, mix 1/3 cup sugar and cinnamon. Add all biscuit pieces to sugar-cinnamon mixture and shake to coat. Place sugared biscuits into a greased and floured Bundt® pan. In a small saucepan, melt remaining sugar with butter. Add sugar-cinnamon from plastic bag to saucepan. Pour mixture over biscuits. Bake at 350 degrees for 40 to 50 minutes. Remove from pan and serve immediately. Makes 10 servings.

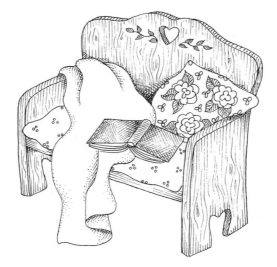

Comfort is...
getting the gingerbread house to stand
after many attempts!

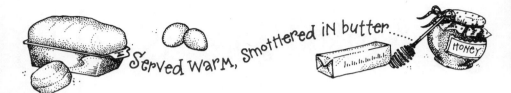

Buttermilk-Cinnamon Bread

Tonya Sheppard
Galveston, TX

*Whenever I'm feeling a little blue, I'll bake this bread! It always
reminds me of times spent with my mother and
grandmother in the kitchen.*

4 c. all-purpose flour	2 c. buttermilk
2 t. baking soda	2 eggs
1 t. salt	1 T. cinnamon
1/2 c. oil	1 to 2 T. walnuts, finely chopped
2-1/2 c. sugar, divided	

In a large mixing bowl, combine flour, baking soda and salt. In a
small bowl, combine oil and 1-1/2 cups sugar. Add buttermilk and
eggs; mix well. Stir into dry ingredients just until moistened. Fill
2 greased 9"x5" loaf pans about 1/3 full. Combine cinnamon and
remaining sugar; sprinkle half over the batter. Top with remaining
batter and cinnamon-sugar. Swirl batter with a knife. Sprinkle with
nuts. Bake at 350 degrees for 45 to 55 minutes or until a toothpick
inserted in the center comes out clean. Cool in pans for 10 minutes
before removing to a wire rack. Makes 2 loaves.

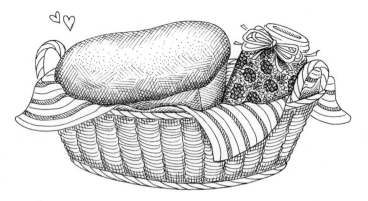

Comfort is...
Dipping your toes in a cool stream.

Cranberry Bread

Cindi Pokorny
Mayville, WI

My Dad's favorite late night snack was toasted cranberry bread...mmm!

2 c. all-purpose flour
1 c. sugar
2 t. baking powder
1/2 t. baking soda
1 t. salt
2 T. orange zest

1/2 c. orange juice
1/2 c. water
1 egg, beaten
2 T. oil
2 c. cranberries, halved

In a large bowl, sift together flour, sugar, baking powder, baking soda and salt. In a separate bowl, combine orange zest, juice, water, egg and oil. Add liquid mixture all at once to dry ingredients; stir until moistened. Fold in cranberries. Turn into a greased and floured 9"x5" pan. Bake at 350 degrees for one hour to one hour and 10 minutes. Makes one loaf.

Comfort is...
A summertime meal made entirely from your own garden...tomatoes, lettuce, green beans and potatoes.

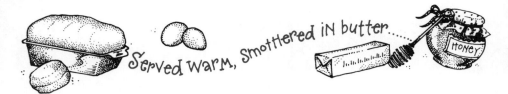

Served warm, smothered in butter......

Pumpkin Bread

Dottie Freeland
Cedar Falls, IA

I made this a lot when my kids were in grade school. Since it makes 3 loaves, I could keep one at home and send the other 2 to school for various bake sales.

3-1/3 c. all-purpose flour
3 c. sugar
2 t. baking soda
1 t. nutmeg
2 t. cinnamon
1-1/2 t. salt

1/2 t. ginger
1 c. oil
2/3 c. cold water
4 eggs
2 c. canned pumpkin

Mix all dry ingredients in a large bowl until completely blended. Make a well in the center of dry ingredients. Pour in oil, water, then eggs and pumpkin. Beat with mixer until smooth and well blended. Pour into 3 greased 9"x5" loaf pans. Bake at 350 degrees for 45 minutes to one hour. Makes 3 loaves.

Cold Tea Gingerbread

Michelle Campen
Peoria, IL

The molasses and tea in this bread make it extra special.

1/2 c. butter
1/2 c. sugar
1 t. baking soda
1/2 c. molasses

1-3/4 c. all-purpose flour
1/2 c. cold tea
1 egg

Cream together butter and sugar. Add baking soda, molasses, flour and tea; beat in egg. Pour into greased and floured 9"x5" loaf pan. Bake at 350 degrees for 40 minutes. Makes one loaf.

Country Biscuits

Krista Jackson
Ava, MO

The key to these biscuits is not overhandling them. They will be tall, fluffy and moist if you don't knead too much!

2 c. all-purpose flour	1/8 t. salt
3 t. baking soda	4 T. shortening
1 t. baking powder	1 c. buttermilk

In a large bowl, mix flour, baking soda, baking powder and salt together. Cut in shortening until crumbly. Add buttermilk and mix thoroughly. Turn out onto a floured counter or board; knead until dough just holds together. Pat out to about 1/2-inch thick. Cut with biscuit cutter or cut into squares with a floured knife. Bake at 425 degrees for 12 to 15 minutes. Makes 8 to 12 biscuits.

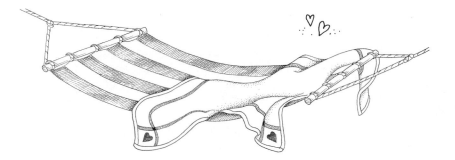

Comfort is...
An afternoon nap in a hammock.

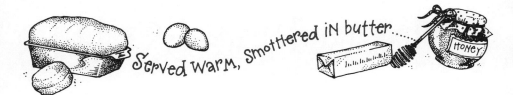

Flowerpot Loaves

Stephanie Mayer
Portsmouth, VA

*Try these for your next garden party...you'll be
the talk of the town!*

2 pkgs. active dry yeast
1-1/2 c. warm water
1/2 c. milk
3 T. sugar
3 T. butter

2 t. salt
5-1/2 to 6 c. all-purpose flour,
  divided
1/2 c. grated Parmesan cheese
1 T. butter, melted

Season pots before preparing bread loaves. Using hot water, without soap, wash and dry twelve, 3-inch unglazed terra cotta flowerpots. Thickly coat the inside and rims with shortening, place on a baking sheet and bake at 425 degrees for one hour. While pots are hot, coat again with shortening, then cool for 3 hours. To prepare bread, dissolve yeast in water and let stand for 5 to 10 minutes, or until foamy. In a saucepan, heat milk, sugar, butter and salt over low heat until butter has melted and sugar has dissolved; cool mixture to lukewarm. Combine milk and yeast mixtures and place in a heavy-duty electric mixer fitted with a paddle. Set mixer on low speed and add 4-1/2 cups of flour, 1/2 cup at a time, until dough pulls away and cleans the sides of bowl. Add cheese and enough remaining flour to form a stiff dough. Remove dough from bowl and knead, on a lightly floured surface, until smooth and elastic, about 5 to 10 minutes. Add more flour if dough sticks to surface. Place dough in a large greased bowl, turning once to coat. Cover loosely and let rise in a warm place for one hour, or until double. Coat insides and rims of pots with shortening, cover holes in pot bottoms with aluminum foil; grease foil. Punch dough down and roll into a fat rope. Cut into 12 equal pieces, shape into balls and place one ball in each pot. Cover and let rise until dough is one to 2 inches above rims, about one hour. Place pots on a baking sheet and bake at 425 degrees for 15 minutes. Reduce heat to 350 degrees and bake an additional 5 to 10 minutes or until loaves are golden and sound hollow when tapped. Cover loosely with foil during the last 10 minutes to prevent overbrowning. Remove loaves from pots; place in a turned-off oven for 5 minutes, brush tops with butter. Makes 12 loaves.

Oat, Apple & Raisin Muffins

Donna Zink
Lapeer, MI

Perfect with a warm cup of herbal tea.

1 egg
3/4 c. milk
1 c. raisins
1 apple, peeled, cored and
   chopped
1/2 c. oil
1 c. all-purpose flour

1 c. quick-cooking oats,
   uncooked
1/3 c. sugar
3 t. baking powder
1 t. salt
1 t. nutmeg
2 t. cinnamon
1/4 t. allspice

In a large bowl, beat egg and stir in remaining ingredients until just moistened. Pour into 12 greased muffin cups, 3/4 full. Bake at 400 degrees for 15 to 20 minutes. Serve cool or warm with butter. Makes 12 muffins.

Comfort is...
Floating on your back in a pool and looking up at the bright blue sky.

Festive Three C Bread

Tina Knotts
Gooseberry Patch

I got this recipe from a dear old friend from my home economics class in high school. Whenever I make this, it brings back wonderful memories!

2-1/2 c. all-purpose flour
1 c. sugar
1 t. baking powder
1 t. baking soda
1 t. cinnamon
1/2 t. salt
3 eggs, beaten
1/2 c. oil

1/2 c. milk
2 c. carrot, shredded
3-1/2 oz. can flaked coconut
1/2 c. maraschino cherries, chopped
1/2 c. raisins
1/2 c. chopped pecans

Stir together flour, sugar, baking powder, baking soda, cinnamon and salt. In a separate bowl, combine eggs, oil and milk; add to flour mixture and stir until just blended. Stir in carrot, coconut, cherries, raisins and pecans. Turn into 4 well greased and floured 16-ounce fruit or vegetable cans with labels removed. Bake at 350 degrees for 45 to 50 minutes. Remove from cans; cool thoroughly on rack. Wrap in foil; store in refrigerator. Makes 4 small loaves.

Comfort is...
A tall vase of fragrant sweet peas.

Melt-in-Your-Mouth Pecan Rolls

Tammy Witt
Damascus, MD

These are just right for an afternoon snack on a chilly day!

1/2 c. brown sugar, packed
1/2 c. butter, softened
1/4 c. corn syrup
2 8-oz. tubes refrigerated
   crescent rolls

2/3 c. chopped pecans
1/4 c. sugar
1 t. cinnamon

In a small bowl, combine brown sugar, butter and corn syrup. Spread in 2 greased 8"x8" baking pans; set aside. Unroll each tube of crescent roll dough into a rectangle; seal seams and perforations. Combine pecans, sugar and cinnamon; sprinkle over dough. Roll up, jelly roll-style, starting with the long side; seal edge. Cut each roll into 16 slices. Place cut side down in prepared pans. Bake at 375 degrees for 14 to 18 minutes or until golden brown. Cool in pans for one minute before inverting onto serving plates. Makes 32 rolls.

Comfort is...
Collecting beautiful autumn leaves to carry
with you on your walk home.

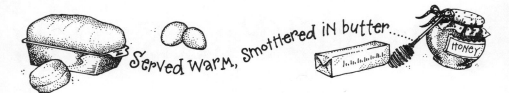

Mini Cinnamon Swirls

Linda Hendrix
Moundville, MO

Perfect with a large glass of chocolate milk...just the right size for dunking!

8-oz. tube refrigerated crescent
   rolls
2 T. butter, softened
2 T. sugar

1 t. cinnamon
1/2 c. powdered sugar
1 T. milk
1/4 t. vanilla extract

Separate dough into 2 rectangles. Spread with butter. Combine sugar and cinnamon; sprinkle over dough. Roll up from narrow end to enclose filling; press edges to seal. Cut each roll into 6 slices. Place in muffin cups coated with non-stick vegetable spray. Bake at 375 degrees for 10 to 15 minutes or until golden brown. Remove to a wire rack. For glaze, combine all remaining ingredients in bowl; mix until smooth. Drizzle over warm rolls. Makes 12.

Comfort is...
Reminiscing over old photos.

Soft Bread Pretzels

Lisa Cook
Amherst, WI

These are a very easy project for kids of all ages...try shaping them into long bread sticks or even letter shapes. Be creative!

1 pkg. active dry yeast	4 c. all-purpose flour
1-1/2 c. warm water	1 egg, beaten
1 T. sugar	coarse salt to taste
1 t. salt	

Dissolve yeast in water in mixing bowl. Add sugar and salt. Blend in flour. Knead the dough on a lightly floured surface until smooth. Cut dough into 10 to 12 pieces. Roll each into a long rope. Twist into pretzel shape or desired shape. Arrange pretzels on a greased baking sheet. Brush tops with egg. Sprinkle coarse salt on top. Bake at 425 degrees for about 15 minutes or until brown. Makes 10 to 12.

Simple Spoon Bread

Dana Cunningham
Lafayette, LA

A perfect recipe for the beginning baker!

1 c. cornmeal	1 t. salt
3 c. milk, divided	3 T. butter, melted
3 eggs, beaten	1 T. baking powder

Bring cornmeal and 2 cups milk to a boil in a medium saucepan over medium heat; stir often. Remove from heat and add remaining milk, eggs and salt; mix well. Add butter and baking powder; mix well. Place in a greased 9"x5" loaf dish. Bake at 350 degrees for 45 minutes. Makes 4 to 6 servings.

Comfort is...
Holding hands with mittens on.

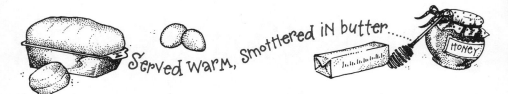

Served Warm, Smothered in butter....

Sesame Seed Muffins

Michelle Adams
South Amherst, OH

Moist and tasty!

2 c. all-purpose flour
1/4 c. sesame seeds
1/2 t. salt
1/4 t. baking soda
1/2 c. butter, softened

3/4 c. sugar
2 eggs
3/4 c. sour cream
1-1/2 t. vanilla extract

Combine flour, sesame seeds, salt and baking soda in a small bowl. In a separate bowl, using an electric mixer, cream butter with sugar until thick and light. Beat in eggs, one at a time. Blend in sour cream and vanilla. Gradually beat in dry ingredients. Place batter into greased muffin tins filling 2/3 full. Bake at 375 degrees for 20 minutes or until tested done. Makes 12 muffins.

Comfort is...
Walking through a toy store and remembering when you were little.

Cream Cheese Muffin Puffs

Dede Smith
Petal, MS

A friend shared this recipe with me. I especially enjoy using it for special breakfasts like birthdays!

1/2 c. sugar
1 t. cinnamon
1/8 t. almond extract
1/4 c. margarine, melted

1/2 t. vanilla extract
10-oz. tube refrigerated biscuits
12 oz. cream cheese, cubed

Combine sugar, cinnamon and almond extract. In a separate bowl, combine margarine and vanilla. Press biscuits into 3-inch circles. Dip each cream cheese cube in margarine mixture, then in sugar mixture. Place cube on center of biscuit, fold dough over cheese; seal well. Dip each filled biscuit into margarine mixture, then sugar mixture. Place seam side down in ungreased muffin pan. Bake at 375 degrees for 12 to 18 minutes; serve warm. Makes 10 to 12.

Comfort is...
Laughing through tears.

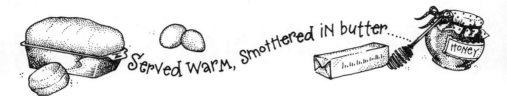

Streusel Biscuits

Kathy Grashoff
Ft. Wayne, IN

These biscuits are a perfect addition to any meal!

2-1/4 c. all-purpose flour
2 t. baking powder
1/2 t. salt
1/2 t. baking soda
1/4 c. chilled shortening

1-1/4 c. plain yogurt
1/4 c. brown sugar, packed
1 t. cinnamon
1/4 t. nutmeg

Stir flour, baking powder, salt and baking soda together in a large bowl; cut in shortening with 2 knives until crumbly. Stir in yogurt. Gather dough into a ball. Place on a lightly floured surface. Knead gently 8 times; pat to a 1/2-inch thickness. Cut with a 2-inch floured cookie cutter. In a medium bowl, stir brown sugar, cinnamon and nutmeg. Press cinnamon mixture on top of each biscuit. Place biscuits on an ungreased baking sheet. Bake at 400 degrees for 15 to 18 minutes. Makes 20 biscuits.

Comfort is...
Decorating the Christmas tree with your family.

Apricot Daisy Bread

Heather Smith
Visalia, CA

Best served with homemade preserves!

3 to 3-1/2 c. all-purpose flour
1 pkg. active dry yeast
3/4 c. milk
1/4 c. butter
2 T. sugar
1 t. salt

2 eggs
1/2 c. apricot preserves
2 T. chopped nuts
3 T. hot water
2-1/2 c. powdered sugar

Combine 1-1/2 cups flour and yeast in a large bowl. In a saucepan, heat milk, butter, sugar and salt until warm. Add flour mixture and eggs to saucepan. Beat for 3 minutes at high speed. Using a spoon, stir in as much of the remaining flour that you can. Turn out onto lightly floured surface; knead in remaining flour to make a moderately stiff dough. Continue kneading until smooth and elastic. Place in a greased bowl. Cover and let rise until double; punch down. Cover and let rest for 10 minutes and transfer to a greased baking sheet. Roll out to a 14-inch circle, place drinking glass in center, make 4 cuts in the dough at equal intervals, from outside of circle to the glass. In same manner, cut each section into 5 strips, making 20 total. Twist 2 strips together. Repeat making 10 twists; pinch ends. Remove glass, remove one twist; coil and place in center of dough. Coil remaining twists to center to create a daisy design. Let rise until double. Bake at 375 degrees for 20 to 25 minutes. Combine apricot preserves and nuts; spread evenly on top of bread. Makes 8 to 12 servings.

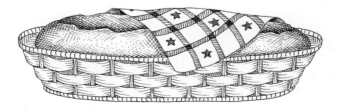

Comfort is...
a double rainbow...and it's still raining!

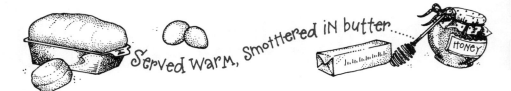

Boston Brown Bread

Barbara Tuve
Montvale, NJ

This is a terrific and easy brown bread recipe. No need for steaming, simple to do and good results everytime!

3 c. whole-wheat flour
2 t. baking soda
1 T. salt
2 c. brown sugar, packed

2 eggs, separated and divided
2 c. buttermilk
1/2 to 3/4 c. raisins

In a large bowl, combine flour, baking soda and salt. Add brown sugar, egg yolks and buttermilk. Stir in raisins and gently fold in egg whites. Fill three greased 1-lb. coffee cans 1/2 full. Bake at 350 degrees for 45 minutes. Cool slightly and remove from cans. Makes 3 loaves.

Comfort is...
    playing with a fluffy, little kitty.

Aunt Dawn's Rolls

Jenny Lyn Day
Marceline, MO

My husband's Aunt Dawn used to make these for any special get-together. Plan to make extras...they don't usually last very long!

2 pkgs. active dry yeast
1/2 c. warm water
2 c. hot water
1/2 c. sugar

3 T. butter
3 t. salt
6 to 6-1/2 c. all-purpose flour
1 stick butter, melted

Dissolve yeast in warm water; set aside. In a large bowl, pour the hot water over sugar, butter and salt; add 2 cups flour and beat as hard as possible. Let cool to lukewarm. Add the yeast mixture and remaining flour. On a lightly floured surface, knead well and let rise until double, about 1-1/2 hours. Knead once again and shape into twenty-four, 1-1/2 inch rolls. Let rise again until double. Place on a greased baking sheet. Bake at 375 degrees for 20 minutes. Spread melted butter over the tops of rolls. Makes 24 rolls.

Comfort is...
The smell of sweet clover from a nearby field.

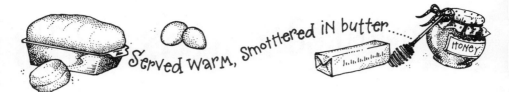

Ginger Hot Rolls

Ginger Griffith
Ravenna, TX

My husband could eat a whole pan of these by himself...if I'd let him!

1 c. milk
1/3 c. shortening
1/2 c. sugar
1-1/2 t. salt

1 cake yeast
1/2 c. lukewarm water
4 c. all-purpose flour, divided

In a saucepan, heat milk and add shortening, sugar and salt; let cool to lukewarm. In a separate bowl, mix yeast and water together; combine with 2 cups flour. Beat yeast mixture into milk mixture until smooth. Add remaining flour and pour all into a large greased bowl. Let rise until double. Shape into rolls and let rise in a warm place for one hour. Bake at 350 degrees for 15 to 20 minutes or until brown. Makes 12 to 16 rolls.

Comfort is...
Coming home on a winter afternoon
and building a cozy fire.

Irish Soda Bread

Tina Kutchman
Johnstown, PA

This recipe is quick, easy and delicious. My kind of recipe!

1-1/2 c. all-purpose flour	1/2 t. salt
1 c. whole-wheat flour	1 c. raisins
1 t. baking soda	1-1/2 c. buttermilk

Combine flours, baking soda and salt in a large mixing bowl. Stir in raisins. Add buttermilk and stir just until dry ingredients are moistened. Turn dough onto lightly floured surface and knead gently for about one minute. Quickly shape into an 8-inch circle and place on a greased baking sheet. Bake at 425 degrees about 40 minutes or until golden. Transfer to a wire rack. Serve warm. Makes one loaf.

Comfort is...
Flannel sheets on a chilly January night.

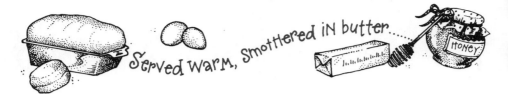

Banana-Chocolate Chip Bread

Bobbi Carney
Aurora, CO

I like to give this bread as a gift to friends, neighbors and teachers!

3/4 c. butter, softened
1-1/2 c. sugar
3 eggs
3 bananas, mashed
3 c. all-purpose flour

1-1/2 t. baking soda
10-oz. can maraschino cherries,
    1/4 c. juice reserved
6-oz. pkg. chocolate chips

In a large bowl, mix all ingredients together. Pour into 2 greased 9"x5" loaf pans. Bake at 350 degrees for one hour. Makes 2 loaves.

Sunshine Muffins

Ellie Bauman
San Anselmo, CA

My children and I love making these sweet mini muffins.
The only problem...they disappear very quickly!

4 T. butter, softened
1 c. sugar, divided
1 egg
2 c. all-purpose flour
4 t. baking powder

1/2 t. salt
1/2 t. nutmeg
1 c. milk
2 t. cinnamon
1/2 c. butter, melted

Beat softened butter and 1/2 cup sugar together until well blended; beat in egg. In a separate bowl, combine flour, baking powder, salt and nutmeg together. Stir flour mixture into butter mixture alternately with milk; blend thoroughly. Pour batter into 1-1/2 inch mini muffin cups filling each 2/3 full. Bake at 375 degrees for 20 minutes; remove from pan. In a mixing bowl, combine remaining sugar and cinnamon; set aside. While still hot, dip each muffin entirely into melted butter and roll in cinnamon-sugar mixture. Makes 12 muffins.

Bread Bowls

Lynn Williams
Muncie, IN

*These bowls are the absolute best for serving
hearty stews and even chili!*

16-oz. pkg. hot roll mix
1 c. instant mashed potato
　　flakes, uncooked
2 T. dried, minced onion

1-1/3 c. hot water
2 T. butter, melted
1 egg

Combine hot roll mix, potato flakes and onion in a large mixing bowl.
Add water, butter and egg, stirring until soft dough forms. Turn onto a
lightly floured surface and knead until dough becomes smooth and
elastic. Cover and let rest for 5 minutes. On a large baking sheet,
invert six, 10-ounce oven-proof custard cups. Coat outside of custard
cups with non-stick vegetable spray. Divide dough into 6 equal balls
and smooth one dough ball over outside of each custard cup. Coat
dough with non-stick vegetable spray and let rise for 30 minutes.
Bake bowls at 375 degrees for 20 to 30 minutes or until golden
brown; cool for 5 minutes. While still warm, carefully remove bread
from custard cups and cool completely. Makes 6 bread bowls.

Comfort is...
　　Blowing out all your birthday candles!

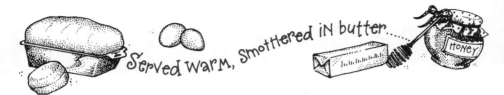

Served warm, Smothered in butter...

Bishop's Bread

Kay Demaso
Revere, MA

This is such a pretty bread...and not too sweet. Tasty year 'round!

1-1/2 c. all-purpose flour
1-1/2 t. baking powder
1/4 t. salt
6-oz. pkg. semi-sweet chocolate
   chips
1 c. chopped walnuts

1 c. flaked coconut
10-oz. jar maraschino cherries,
   drained and halved
3 eggs, beaten
1 c. sugar

In a large bowl, sift together flour, baking powder and salt. In a separate bowl, mix together chocolate chips, walnuts, coconut and cherries; add to dry ingredients. In a mixing bowl, beat eggs together with sugar; stir into flour mixture, blend well. Spread batter evenly in a greased and floured 9"x5" pan. Bake at 325 degrees for one to 1-1/2 hours. Wrap in foil and serve the next day. Makes one loaf.

Comfort is...
   Warm and gooey chocolate chip cookies.

Banana Cream Muffins

Marla Arbet
Burlington, WI

Light, creamy and delicious muffins. My kids eat them up!

1/4 c. margarine, softened
3-oz. pkg. cream cheese,
  softened
1/4 c. applesauce
3/4 c. brown sugar, packed
3 bananas, mashed
2 egg whites, beaten

1/4 c. sour cream
1 c. all-purpose flour
1/2 c. whole-wheat flour
3/4 c. mini chocolate chips
1 t. baking soda
1 t. baking powder
1/2 c. chopped nuts

In a large bowl, cream margarine, cream cheese, applesauce and brown sugar together. Add bananas, egg whites and sour cream; mix thoroughly. In a separate bowl, combine remaining ingredients. Make a well in the center of dry ingredients; pour banana mixture into the well. Mix until combined. Pour batter into 18 greased muffin cups filling 3/4 full. Bake at 325 degrees for 20 to 25 minutes. Makes 18 muffins.

Comfort is...
Remembering your first kiss.

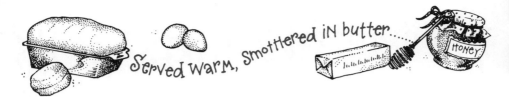

Served warm, Smothered in butter... HONEY

Orange-Cinnamon Swirl Bread

Patty Rogers
Chicago, IL

A perfect pick-me-up on those cold, windy and dreary days!

5-1/2 c. all-purpose flour,
   divided
2 pkgs. instant active yeast
1/3 c. dry powdered milk
1 c. sugar, divided
1-1/2 t. salt
1-1/4 c. hot water
1/4 c. butter, softened

1 T. plus 1 t. orange zest,
   divided
3/4 c. plus 4 t. orange juice,
   divided
1 egg
1 T. cinnamon
1 c. powdered sugar

Measure 2 cups flour into a large mixing bowl and add yeast, dry
milk, 1/2 cup sugar and salt. Pour in hot water and blend into a
thin batter. Add butter, one tablespoon orange zest, 3/4 cup orange
juice and egg. Add remaining flour, 1/4 cup at a time, until dough
forms a ball that comes away from the sides of the bowl. Knead for
8 minutes. Place dough in a greased bowl and cover tightly with
plastic wrap. Let rise for 45 minutes. Fold back plastic wrap and punch
dough down. Turn onto a floured surface and divide into 2 pieces. Roll
each piece into a 15"x7" rectangle. In a small bowl, combine remaining
sugar and cinnamon; spread each dough half with mixture. Roll from
narrow side and pinch seams together. Place in 2 greased 9"x5" loaf
pans, cover with wax paper and let rise for 45 minutes. Bake at
375 degrees for 10 minutes and then reduce oven to 325 degrees
for 30 minutes. In a large bowl, blend together powdered sugar,
remaining orange zest and orange juice; set aside. Remove from
oven, turn onto wire rack and let cool. Spread frosting over the top.
Makes 2 loaves.

Comfort is...
Inviting your sisters over for brunch.

Lemon-Raspberry Crumb Muffins

Linda Hendrix
Moundville, MO

These are the BEST muffins!

2-1/4 c. all-purpose flour,
   divided
1/2 c. plus 1/3 c. sugar, divided
2 t. baking powder
1/2 t. baking soda
1/2 t. salt

8-oz. carton lemon yogurt
1/2 c. oil
1 t. lemon zest
2 eggs
1 to 1-1/2 c. raspberries
2 T. butter

In a large bowl, combine 2 cups flour, 1/2 cup sugar, baking powder, baking soda and salt. In a small bowl, combine yogurt, oil, lemon zest and eggs. Add to dry ingredients; stir just until dry ingredients are moistened. Gently stir in raspberries. Coat muffin pans with non-stick vegetable spray and fill 3/4 full. Combine remaining flour, sugar and butter with a pastry blender or fork until crumbly. Sprinkle topping over batter. Bake at 400 degrees for 18 to 20 minutes. Makes 12 muffins.

Comfort is...
   picking fresh strawberries with your mom.

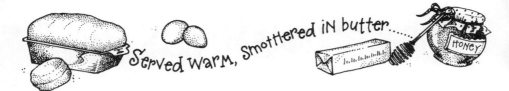

Served warm, smothered in butter....

Molasses-Raisin Bread

Marsha Dunster
Granville, NY

This recipe was my great grandmother Ida's. The original recipe is dated 1920!

1 c. molasses
2 eggs
2 c. milk
2 c. sour milk
5 c. graham flour

3 c. all-purpose flour
4 t. baking soda
3/4 c. sugar
6-oz. pkg. raisins

Mix molasses, eggs and milks together; add dry ingredients and raisins. Pour into 4 greased and floured 9"x5" loaf pans. Bake at 350 degrees for 40 to 45 minutes. Makes 4 loaves.

Twisty Rolls

Debi Gilpin
Bluefield, WV

I have been making these for years...but my dear Aunt Betty will always be the undisputed world champion Twisty Roll maker!

1 pkg. active dry yeast
1/4 c. warm water
1/4 c. butter, softened
3 T. sugar
2 t. salt

3/4 c. milk, scalded
2 eggs, beaten and divided
3-1/2 c. all-purpose flour
1 c. powdered sugar
2 to 3 T. milk

Dissolve yeast in water; set aside. In a saucepan, heat butter, sugar, salt and scalded milk; mix well and cool to lukewarm. Add one egg and yeast mixture; blend in flour. Knead until smooth, place in greased bowl and let rise in warm place until double, about one to 1-1/2 hours. Punch down and roll out to a 1/4-inch thickness. Cut into strips, about 1/2-inch by 6-inches and braid 3 strips together to form a roll. Place on a baking sheet and brush with remaining egg. Let rise an additional 30 minutes. Bake at 400 degrees for 12 to 15 minutes. Blend together powdered sugar and milk until a glaze consistency. When cool, frost. Makes 2 dozen.

Ice Box Gingerbread

Becky Newton
Oklahoma City, OK

When my mother used to make these when I was little, we would always sneak spoonfuls of the batter!

1 c. butter
1 c. molasses
1 c. sugar
4 eggs, beaten
1/2 c. chopped walnuts
1/2 c. raisins
1 c. buttermilk

2 t. baking soda
4 c. all-purpose flour
1/2 t. allspice
1 t. ginger
1 t. nutmeg
1 t. cinnamon

In a large bowl, cream butter, molasses and sugar together; add eggs, walnuts, raisins, buttermilk and baking soda. In a separate bowl, sift together flour and spices; gradually add to butter mixture. Stir well, cover and place in refrigerator. Pour batter 2/3 full into muffin tins coated with non-stick vegetable spray. Bake at 350 degrees for 35 to 40 minutes. Serve warm. Makes 48.

Comfort is...
Homemade, handcranked ice cream.

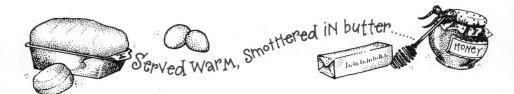

Served warm, smothered in butter...

Golden Raisin-Honey Loaf

Carol Hickman
Kingsport, TN

This bread is scrumptious!

2-1/2 c. all-purpose flour
1/3 c. brown sugar, packed
2 t. baking powder
1 t. salt
1/2 t. baking soda
1/2 c. butter-flavored shortening

1 c. golden raisins
2 eggs
1/2 c. milk
1/2 c. honey
2 t. lemon zest

In a large bowl, combine flour, sugar, baking powder, salt and baking soda. With a pastry blender or 2 knives, cut in shortening until mixture resembles coarse crumbs. Stir in raisins. In a small bowl, beat eggs, milk, honey and lemon zest together. Stir honey mixture into dry ingredients, just until moistened. Spoon into a greased and floured 9"x5" loaf pan. Bake at 325 degrees for 50 minutes or until toothpick inserted comes out clean. Cool in pan for 10 minutes. Remove from pan and cool bread completely on wire rack. Wrap in plastic wrap and let stand overnight before slicing. Makes one loaf.

Comfort is...

Waking up in the middle of the night and realizing you still have a few more hours to sleep.

Cornbread Bowls

Elizabeth Ramicone
Dublin, OH

A quick and easy way to make soup bowls!

11-1/2 oz. tube refrigerated
cornbread twists

Coat a baking sheet with butter-flavored non-stick vegetable spray. Invert two 8-ounce custard cups several inches apart on baking sheet, coat outside of cups with cooking spray. Separate cornbread twists at perforations. Flatten each strip to 2-inches wide. Cover the outside of one custard cup with half of strips, cutting away the excess and moistening edge to seal strips together. Repeat procedure with remaining cornbread strips and custard cup. Bake at 400 degrees for 10 to 12 minutes. Cool on wire rack. Remove bowls from custard cups. Makes two, 10-ounce bowls.

Comfort is...
The sound of crickets on a warm summer night.

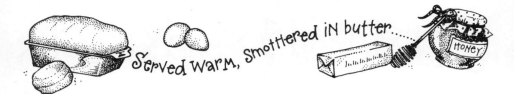

Sweet Lemon Bread

Pat Habiger
Spearville, KS

This bread always reminds me of summer and lemonade!

1 c. butter, softened
3 c. sugar, divided
4 eggs
1/2 t. salt
1/2 t. baking soda

3 c. all-purpose flour
1 c. buttermilk
zest of one lemon
1 c. chopped pecans
juice of 3 lemons

In a large bowl, cream butter with 2 cups sugar. Add eggs, one at a time, beating well after each addition. In a separate bowl, sift together salt, baking soda and flour. Add to sugar mixture alternately with buttermilk. Stir in lemon zest and pecans. Pour into 2 greased and floured 9"x5" loaf pans. Bake at 325 degrees for one hour. While bread bakes, mix lemon juice and remaining sugar together; stir until sugar is dissolved. When bread is done, turn onto wax paper and spoon glaze over top while bread is still hot. Makes 2 loaves.

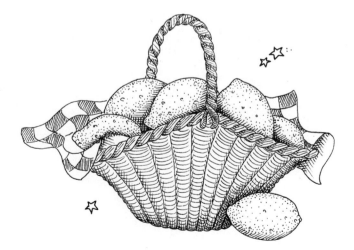

Comfort is...
a baked apple with cinnamon, nuts and raisins!

Strawberry Surprise Biscuits

Cheri Henry
Newalla, OK

*Take your family to a strawberry farm to pick
your own strawberries. What fun!*

2 c. all-purpose flour
2 T. sugar
3 t. baking powder
1/2 t. salt
1/4 c. margarine

3/4 c. plus 1-1/2 t. milk, divided
12 strawberries
1/3 c. powdered sugar
1/8 t. vanilla extract

Whisk together flour, sugar, baking powder and salt. Cut in margarine with pastry blender or 2 knives until crumbly. Stir in 3/4 cup milk until just moistened. Knead lightly in bowl to work in loose flour. Divide dough into 12 pieces. Pat each piece into a 3-inch circle on a floured surface. Center a strawberry on each circle. Bring dough edges up over strawberry; pinch to seal. Bake on non-stick baking sheet at 425 degrees for 18 to 20 minutes, or until golden brown. Blend together remaining ingredients for glaze. Cool biscuits and drizzle with glaze. Makes 12 biscuits.

Comfort is...
*A well stocked pantry with a
snow storm on its way!*

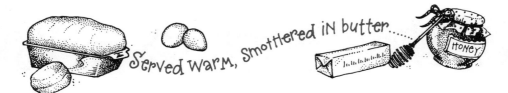

Served warm, smothered in butter......

Corn Fritters

Sharon Tillman
Hampton, VA

Whenever my mother comes to visit, she always asks me if I'd like her to make these for me. They remind me of my sweet childhood!

1 T. sugar
1/8 t. salt
1 c. milk
1/2 c. cornmeal
1 T. butter
1 t. lemon zest

1 egg yolk
1 egg, beaten
1/4 c. fine bread crumbs
oil
Garnish: maple syrup

Add sugar, salt and milk to a double boiler; bring mixture to a boil. Slowly add cornmeal, stirring, constantly. Bring to a boil again and simmer 20 minutes. Remove from heat; stir in butter, lemon zest and egg yolk. Carefully pour mixture on a lightly dampened surface and roll to 1/2-inch thickness; cool and cut into squares. Dip each square in egg, then in bread crumbs. Add enough oil to a deep skillet or Dutch oven to equal 2 inches. Heat oil and cook corn fritters until golden brown. Drain and serve with maple syrup. Makes 8 to 12.

Comfort is...
The smell of earth after a soft rain.

Cheddary Cheese Crackers

Gail Prather
Bethel, MN

What fun to have homemade crackers!

1/2 c. sharp Cheddar cheese,
  grated
1/2 c. all-purpose flour
2 T. butter
1/4 t. salt

1/8 t. paprika
1/8 t. cayenne pepper
2 T. cold water
1/2 t. Kosher salt

Mix all ingredients, except Kosher salt together in a bowl. Shape into a roll 1-1/2 inches wide. Chill at least 2 hours wrapped in wax paper. Cut into thin slices to make one dozen or more crackers. Roll out onto a lightly floured board and cut into desired shape. Top with Kosher salt. Bake on an ungreased baking sheet at 425 degrees for 12 to 15 minutes until lightly brown. Makes one dozen crackers.

Comfort is...
*Seeing spring flowers peeking up
through the ground.*

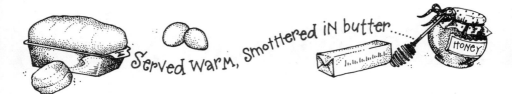

Served warm, Smothered iN butter... HONEY

Cheese Bread Bowls

Tina Wright
Atlanta, GA

*I remember my mom making these for us...it was such fun to eat
the yummy soup and be able to nibble on the bowl!*

4 to 4-1/2 c. all-purpose flour,
   divided
1 pkg. active dry yeast
1-1/2 c. milk
1 T. sugar

1 t. salt
2 c. Cheddar cheese, shredded
1 egg yolk
1 T. water

Blend together 2 cups flour and yeast; set aside. Heat milk, sugar and
salt until warm, add milk mixture and cheese to flour mixture. Using a
mixer on low speed; beat for 30 seconds. Increase mixer speed to high
and continue to beat for 3 minutes. Add in enough remaining flour
until dough is no longer sticky. Turn on a lightly floured surface and
knead for 6 to 8 minutes, then place in greased bowl, turning once to
coat all the sides. Cover and let rise until double, about 1-1/2 hours.
Punch dough down and divide into 8 portions. Shape each portion in
a ball, cover and let rise for 10 minutes. Roll each ball in a 6-inch
circle, then coat the outsides only of 8 custard cups with non-stick
vegetable spray. Turn the cups upside down and smooth dough over
each to form a bowl. Set cups on a baking sheet and bake at
375 degrees for 10 minutes. In a small bowl, whisk together egg yolk
and water. Carefully remove baking sheet from oven and gently slide
each bread bowl from cup. Brush the inside of each baked bowl with
egg yolk mixture and return to oven for 5 additional minutes. Turn
oven off and leave bread bowls in oven until a light golden brown.
Makes 8 edible bowls.

Comfort is...
Following your heart.

mmmmm

Gooey Sweet Treats

Cookies baking & pie crusts browning,
Yummy baked goodies that are meant
to be shared
with those
you
love most.

Strawberry Shortcake

Cindy Edmondson
Red Creek, NY

*This is my grandmother's recipe. Grandma is now 96 and still enjoys
her strawberry shortcake...it's a family tradition!*

1-1/2 c. all-purpose flour	1/2 c. milk
1/4 t. salt	1/8 c. sugar
2 t. baking powder	Garnish: strawberries, sliced and
1/4 c. shortening	whipped topping
1 egg, beaten	

In a large bowl, sift together flour, salt and baking powder; cut in
shortening. In a separate bowl, combine egg and milk and add all at
once to the flour mix; mix lightly. Pat into an 8"x8" pan and sprinkle
with sugar. Bake at 400 degrees for 12 to 15 minutes. Top will be
lightly browned. Serve with strawberries and whipped topping. Makes
8 to 10 servings.

Comfort is...
*A slice of warm apple pie topped with
vanilla ice cream.*

Blueberry Buckle

Maria McGovern
Stratford, NJ

This is an old fashioned, easy to prepare recipe, just like Grandma used to make!

1-1/4 c. sugar, divided
1/4 c. shortening
1 egg, beaten
1 c. milk
2 c. all-purpose flour

3/4 t. salt
2 t. baking powder
1/2 c. butter, melted and divided
1 pt. blueberries
2-1/2 t. cinnamon

Cream together 3/4 cup sugar and shortening. Beat in egg and milk. Add flour, one cup at a time. Add salt, baking powder and 1/4 cup butter. Stir in blueberries and spread mixture into a greased 13"x9" pan. In a small bowl, combine remaining sugar, cinnamon and butter; sprinkle over top of cake. Bake at 350 degrees for 35 minutes. Makes 10 to 12 servings.

Comfort is...

getting your favorite magazine in the mail!

Mom's Graham Cracker Cookies

Margaret Scoresby
Mount Vernon, OH

So quick, easy and delicious!

15 graham crackers, divided
1 c. brown sugar, packed
1 c. flaked coconut
1 c. graham cracker crumbs

1/2 c. butter
1/2 c. milk
1/8 t. salt

Line a 13"x9" pan with whole graham crackers. Combine remaining ingredients in a saucepan and boil for 10 minutes. Remove from oven and spread over crackers. Add a second layer of graham crackers over filling. Top with icing. Cut into squares to serve. Makes 12 to 14 cookies.

Icing:

4. c. powdered sugar
5 T. butter, melted

3 T. heavy cream
1 t. vanilla extract

Blend all ingredients together until smooth.

Comfort is...
Licking the brownie batter from the bowl!

Apple Fritters

Loretta Coney
LaGrange, IN

This recipe is a favorite at our apple festival!

2 T. sugar
2 c. all-purpose flour
2 t. baking powder
1/2 t. salt
2 T. dry powdered milk
1/2 t. cinnamon

2 eggs
1 to 1-1/2 c. water
2 T. oil
2 c. apples, peeled, cored and
   chopped
Garnish: powdered sugar

Combine sugar, flour, baking powder, salt, powdered milk and cinnamon together. Add in eggs, water, oil and apples; mix well. Drop by tablespoonfuls into hot oil until brown, about 5 minutes. After cooled, roll in powdered sugar to coat. Makes approximately 2 dozen.

Comfort is...
   Warm slices of banana bread.

Whoopie Pies

Gena-Marie Nuffer
Surprise, AZ

For a tasty variation during the holiday season, add crushed bits of candy cane to the cake dough as it's being mixed...yummy!

1-1/2 c. shortening, divided
2 c. sugar
4 egg whites, whisked and
    divided
1 t. salt
1 c. sour cream
2 t. baking soda

4 t. vanilla extract, divided
1 c. baking cocoa
1 c. hot water
4 c. plus 4 t. all-purpose flour,
    divided
4 c. powdered sugar, divided

In a large bowl, cream together one cup shortening and sugar. Add 2 egg whites, salt, sour cream, baking soda, 2 teaspoons vanilla, baking cocoa, water and 4 cups flour. Blend until thoroughly mixed. The dough will be rather sticky and goopy and a little lumpy. Spoon out 2-inch balls of dough onto baking sheets, making sure that the balls do not touch and that there are an even number. Bake at 375 degrees for 15 minutes or until a toothpick comes out clean; cool completely. For filling, combine remaining egg whites, vanilla and flour; mix well. Add 2 cups powdered sugar and remaining shortening to egg white mixture; combine well. Add in remaining powdered sugar; mix well. When all ingredients are thoroughly combined and cakes are cooled, generously frost cake on the flat side and place another cake on top, flat sides facing each other. Wrap each whoopie pie individually to maintain freshness. Refrigerate. Makes 10 to 12.

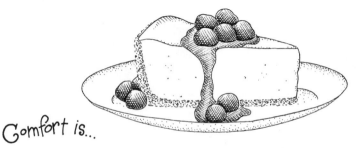

Comfort is...

Your favorite aunt's homemade cheesecake.

Gooey Sweet Treats

Mocha Devils Torte

Mary Rita Schlagel
Warwick, NY

For variety, slice this loaf cake, place a scoop of ice cream on top, drizzle with some hot fudge sauce and top with a strawberry!

1 c. black coffee, cooled
2 eggs
1/4 c. plus 1 to 2 T. milk, divided
1/4 c. sour cream
18-1/4 oz. pkg. devils food cake mix
1/2 c. chocolate chips

21-oz. can cherry or strawberry pie filling
8 oz. whipped topping
3-1/2 oz. pkg. instant vanilla pudding mix
1 t. almond extract
Garnish: chocolate chips and jimmies

In a large bowl, place coffee, eggs, 1/4 cup milk and sour cream. Beat with an electric mixer until frothy. Add in dry cake mix and blend until ingredients are combined. Pour 1/2 of the batter into each of 2, greased 9"x5" loaf pans. Sprinkle chocolate chips over top of batter. Bake at 350 degrees for 30 minutes or when tested done. Remove from oven and let cool for at least one to 2 hours. Remove from pan and with a serrated knife, carefully split each loaf in half horizontally, then fill each half with pie filling. Place layers back on together. In a mixing bowl, combine whipped topping, pudding mix and almond extract, adding remaining milk until frosting consistency. Frost the entire cake. Garnish with chocolate chips and jimmies. Makes 8 servings.

Chocolate Eclair Cake

Karen Slack
Mount Pleasant, TX

*My children always enjoyed having me make this
during their summer vacation.*

2 3-1/2 oz. pkg. instant French
    vanilla pudding mix
3 c. plus 3 T. milk, divided
8 oz. whipped topping
2 1-oz. packets pre-melted
    unsweetened chocolate

1 t. vanilla extract
1-1/2 c. powdered sugar
6 T. margarine, softened
2 T. corn syrup
16-oz. pkg. graham crackers

Mix pudding mixes with 3 cups milk and beat until thickened. Fold in
whipped topping; set aside. Prepare frosting by combining baking
chocolate, vanilla, powdered sugar, remaining milk, margarine and
corn syrup; set aside. Assemble cake in an ungreased 15"x10" pan.
Make 5 layers in pan alternating with graham crackers and pudding,
beginning and ending with graham crackers. Frost before serving.
Makes 14 to 16 servings.

Comfort is...
Dunking cookies in a cold glass of milk.

Raspberry Swirled Brownies

*Pat Habiger
Spearville, KS*

Absolutely delectable!

1 stick butter, softened
1 c. sugar
16-oz. can chocolate syrup
4 eggs
1-1/2 c. all-purpose flour

3-oz. pkg. cream cheese,
  softened
2/3 c. raspberry preserves
1 c. unsweetened raspberries
Garnish: whipped cream and
  raspberries

In a mixing bowl, cream butter and sugar. Add chocolate syrup and eggs; mix well. Add flour; mix well. Beat in cream cheese and preserves until smooth; gently fold raspberries into the batter. Spread in a greased 15"x10" baking pan. Bake at 350 degrees for 30 to 35 minutes. Cut into 2-1/2 inch diamonds. Garnish with whipped cream and raspberries if desired. Makes 2-1/2 dozen.

Comfort is...
Watching and learning from your grandmother
how to make a pie.

Easy Peach Cobbler

Melonie Klosterhoff
Eielson Air Force Base, AK

If they're available...use fresh-from-the-farm
peaches for a special treat!

16-oz. can sliced peaches,
   undrained
1 c. all-purpose flour
1-1/4 c. sugar, divided

1 c. milk
2 t. baking powder
1/8 t. salt
1 stick butter

In a medium saucepan, over medium heat, cook peaches until boiling.
In a medium bowl, mix flour, one cup sugar, milk, baking powder and
salt. In a 2-quart casserole dish, melt butter. Pour batter over butter.
Add peaches; do not stir. Sprinkle remaining sugar over entire
casserole. Bake at 400 degrees for 20 to 30 minutes. Serve with ice
cream or whipped cream. Makes 6 servings.

Comfort is...
Mixing up a batch of chocolate chip cookie dough,
and eating what's stuck to the spoon.

Gooey Sweet Treats

Grandma Miller's Apple Dumplings

Julie Neilson
Charlotte, NC

When I bake these dumplings with my daughters, I am always reminded of baking with my beloved grandmother. They were, and are, such a treat!

2-1/2 c. all-purpose flour
4 t. baking powder
1 t. salt
3/4 c. shortening
1/2 c. milk

6 to 8 apples, peeled and cored
2 c. sugar
2 c. water
1 t. cinnamon

Mix together flour, baking powder, salt, shortening and milk. Roll out pastry, cut into squares large enough to completely cover each apple; place apples in the center of each square and pull corners to the top of apple, pinch to seal. Place dumplings into a 13"x9" pan. In a saucepan, combine sugar, water and cinnamon. Boil on stovetop; cool slightly. Spoon 1/3 of mixture over dumplings. Bake at 350 degrees for 45 minutes to one hour. Spoon sauce over dumplings twice during baking time. Makes 6 to 8 servings.

Comfort is...
The first rosebud blooming on the rosebush you got for Mother's Day.

Pecan Pie Brownies

Kathy Grashoff
Fort Wayne, IN

Take these to your next family picnic...they're always a winner!

2 eggs
1/3 c. water
1/4 c. oil

12-1/2 oz. can pecan pie filling
21-1/2 oz. pkg. brownie mix
1/2 c. chopped pecans

In a large bowl, mix eggs, water, oil and pecan filling until blended. Add brownie mix and mix by hand until blended. Pour into a greased 13"x9" pan. Sprinkle pecans on top. Bake at 350 degrees for 30 to 35 minutes. Cool and then cut into squares. Makes 15 to 20 brownies.

Chocolate Chip Cookies

Christi Miller
New Paris, PA

I LOVE these cookies! I know you will too.

1-1/2 c. butter
1 c. brown sugar, packed
1-1/2 c. sugar
4 eggs
1 T. vanilla extract
1 t. lemon juice
3 c. all-purpose flour
1-1/4 t. salt

2 t. baking soda
1/2 c. long-cooking oats,
  uncooked
2 6-oz. pkgs. chocolate chips
6-oz. pkg. english toffee bits
6-oz. pkg. peanut butter chips
2 c. chopped walnuts
1 t. cinnamon

In a large bowl, beat butter, sugars and eggs for 5 minutes. Add vanilla and lemon juice. Add remaining ingredients. Drop onto a lightly greased baking sheet. Bake at 325 degrees for 15 minutes. Makes 8 dozen.

Gooey Sweet Treats

Shoo Fly Cake

Cheryl Bastian
Northumberland, PA

Yummy and not too sweet!

3 c. all-purpose flour
2 c. sugar
3/4 c. shortening

1 t. baking soda
2 c. boiling water
1 c. molasses

Mix flour, sugar and shortening together; remove 2 cups and set aside for topping. In a separate bowl, mix baking soda with boiling water; add in molasses. Mix molasses mixture into flour mixture. Pour into an ungreased 13"x9" baking pan. Sprinkle the top with the reserved 2 cups of topping. Bake at 350 degrees for 35 to 40 minutes. Makes 20 to 24 servings.

Comfort is...
An extra-special birthday cake with lots and lots of pink icing roses!

Warm Apple-Buttermilk Custard Pie

Susan Helms
Beaver Falls, PA

Creamy and smooth!

1/2 c. plus 3 T. butter, divided
2 c. apples, peeled, cored and
   sliced
1-3/4 c. sugar, divided
3/4 t. cinnamon, divided
4 eggs

1/2 c. plus 2 T. all-purpose flour,
   divided
1 t. vanilla extract
3/4 c. buttermilk
9-inch deep-dish pie crust,
   unbaked
1/4 c. brown sugar, packed
Garnish: whipped topping

Melt 1/4 cup butter in a skillet. Add apples and 1/2 cup sugar;
cook for about 3 minutes or until apples are tender. Add 1/2 teaspoon
cinnamon; set mixture aside to cool. In a mixing bowl, cream together
1/4 cup butter and one cup sugar. Add eggs, one at a time, beating
well after each. Mix in 2 tablespoons flour, vanilla and buttermilk.
Place apple mixture in crust. Pour buttermilk mixture over top. Bake
at 325 degrees for 30 minutes. While pie is baking, prepare topping.
Mix together remaining butter, sugar, brown sugar, flour and
cinnamon until crumbly. After pie has baked, sprinkle topping over
top of pie and return to oven for an additional 30 minutes or until
knife inserted in center comes out clean. Cool for one to 2 hours.
Serve with whipped topping. Makes 8 servings.

Comfort is...
*A basket full of pink geraniums on a
porch shouting "Welcome!"*

Blackberry Cobbler

Sharon Chesley
North East, PA

You can make your own self-rising flour by using 1-1/2 cups all-purpose flour to 1/4 teaspoon salt plus 2-1/4 teaspoons baking powder!

1/2 c. butter, melted
1 c. plus 2 T. sugar, divided
1 c. water
1-1/2 c. self-rising flour

1/2 c. butter
1/3 c. milk, room temperature
2 c. blackberries
1/2 t. cinnamon

Place melted butter in a 9"x9" baking dish. In a saucepan, heat one cup sugar and one cup water until sugar dissolves; set aside. In a separate bowl, cut flour and butter together until coarse crumbs form. Add milk and stir until dough leaves sides of bowl; roll out into a rectangle. Spread dough with berries, sprinkle with cinnamon and roll up jelly roll-style. Cut into 1-1/2 inch slices. Place in pan on top of melted butter. Pour the sugar water over top; bake at 350 degrees for 45 minutes. Remove from oven; sprinkle with remaining sugar and return to oven for 15 additional minutes. Makes 4 to 6 servings.

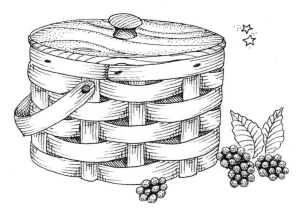

Comfort is...
A slice of warm blackberry pie.

Pineapple Upside-Down Cake

Phyllis Peters
Three Rivers, MI

I received this recipe from a co-worker. It is so simple to make...perfect for the working person!

18-1/4 oz. pkg. yellow cake mix
1 c. brown sugar, packed

20-oz. can sliced pineapple, juice reserved
10-oz. jar maraschino cherries

Prepare cake batter according to directions on package. Spread brown sugar in the bottom of a 13"x9" baking pan, pour pineapple juice over it and arrange the pineapple slices on brown sugar; center a cherry in each pineapple. Evenly pour cake batter over the top. Bake at 350 degrees for 40 minutes or until tested done. Makes 12 to 16 servings.

Comfort is...
The feel of the sun warming the back of your neck as you work in the garden.

Gooey Sweet Treats

Banana Cream Cake

Gail Prather
Bethel, MN

*My dad is a huge banana fan. When I found this recipe I was
sure it would be a hit with him...and I was right!*

1/2 c. shortening
1-3/4 c. plus 2 T. sugar, divided
3 eggs, divided
2 t. vanilla extract, divided
3 c. plus 1 T. all-purpose flour,
   divided
1 t. baking powder
1 t. baking soda
3/4 t. salt, divided

1-1/2 t. cinnamon, divided
1/2 t. nutmeg
1/2 t. cardamom
1/3 c. lemon juice
3 bananas, mashed
1 c. chopped walnuts
2 3-oz. pkgs. cream cheese
2 T. butter, melted

In a mixing bowl, cream together shortening and 1-1/2 cups sugar.
Beat in 2 eggs, one at a time, beating well after each. Add one
teaspoon vanilla; beat well. In a small bowl, sift together 3 cups
flour, baking powder, baking soda, 1/2 teaspoon salt, one teaspoon
cinnamon, nutmeg and cardamom. Beat dry ingredients into the
creamed mixture, alternately with lemon juice, starting and ending
with dry ingredients. Stir in bananas and nuts. To make filling,
combine cream cheese, 1/4 cup sugar, 1/2 teaspoon cinnamon,
1/4 teaspoon salt, remaining egg, flour and vanilla; beat well.
Spread half of the batter into a greased and floured Bundt® pan,
drop the filling over the batter by spoonfuls and then top with the
remaining batter. Bake at 350 degrees for 45 to 50 minutes or until
edges are nicely browned and come away from the sides of the pan.
Cool cake in the pan on a wire rack for 10 minutes; invert onto a wire
rack. Brush cake with the melted butter and sprinkle with the
remaining sugar; allow to cool completely. Makes 12 to 16 servings.

Comfort is...
    Watching bluebirds splashing in a birdbath.

Cherry Crunch

*Andrea Scott
Jacksonville, FL*

A quick alternative to cherry pie!

21-oz. can cherry pie filling
20-oz. can crushed pineapple,
    undrained

18-1/4 oz. pkg. yellow cake mix
1-1/2 sticks butter, sliced
1 c. chopped pecans

Layer ingredients in a greased 13"x9" pan as listed. Bake at 350 degrees for 35 to 45 minutes or until golden brown. Serve warm. Makes 12 to 15 servings.

Warm Turtle Cake

*Larissa Strand
Maple Shade, NJ*

Chocolate cake with a gooey caramel filling and a crunchy pecan topping!

14-oz. pkg. caramels
5-oz. can evaporated milk
18-1/4 oz. pkg. German
    chocolate cake mix with
    pudding

3/4 c. butter
12-oz. pkg. semi-sweet
    chocolate chips
2 c. pecans, divided

In a saucepan, over low heat, heat caramels and milk until caramels are melted. Prepare cake batter according to package directions, except only use 1/2 the oil listed. Add butter and beat on high until batter is thick and smooth. Spread about 3 cups of batter into an aluminum foil-lined and greased 13"x9" pan. Bake at 350 degrees for 12 to 15 minutes or until cake puffs around the edges and the center is slightly wet. Pour the caramel mixture over the cake and spread. Sprinkle with one cup of the chocolate chips and one cup of the pecans. Spoon remaining batter over the top. Bake an additional 35 to 45 minutes, or until cake springs back when gently pressed. Meanwhile, melt the remaining chocolate chips; spread over cake and sprinkle with remaining pecans. Let cool. Makes 12 servings.

Granny Kate's Fudge Pie

Nicole Martin
Maryville, TN

If you love chocolate, you'll love this pie.

1 stick butter
1-oz. square unsweetened
   baking chocolate
1 c. sugar
1/4 t. salt

1/4 c. all-purpose flour
2 eggs
1 t. vanilla extract
9-inch pie crust, unbaked

In a saucepan, melt butter and chocolate over low heat. Stir in sugar, salt, flour, eggs and vanilla; mix well. Pour mixture into pie crust. Bake at 350 degrees for 20 minutes. Let cool for one hour before cutting and serving. Makes 6 to 8 servings.

Comfort is...
Going home to visit and sleeping in your old bed.

Strawberry Cheesecake Trifle

Linda Hendrix
Moundville, MO

This is wonderful! I always get rave reviews when I serve this.

2 to 2-1/2 qts. strawberries,
   sliced
2 to 3 T. sugar
2 to 3 T. plus 1/4 t. almond
   extract, divided
2 8-oz. pkgs. cream cheese,
   softened
1 c. sour cream

2 c. powdered sugar
1 t. vanilla extract
16 oz. whipped topping
1 angel food cake, torn into
   pieces
Garnish: whipped topping and
   strawberries, sliced

Mix strawberries with sugar and 2 to 3 tablespoons almond extract;
set aside. In a separate bowl, mix cream cheese, sour cream, powdered
sugar, vanilla and remaining almond extract; fold in whipped topping.
Layer 1/2 of cake pieces, 1/2 of strawberries and 1/2 of cream cheese
mixture in a large clear glass bowl; repeat layers. Garnish top of trifle
with whipped topping and additional strawberries. Refrigerate before
serving. Makes 20 servings.

Comfort is...
   Warm sugar cut-outs on a snowy winter night.

Banana Split Dessert

Becky Newton
Oklahoma City, OK

A simple way to enjoy a favorite summertime treat!

25 to 30 chocolate sandwich
  cookies, crushed
1/4 c. butter, melted
2 8-oz. pkgs. cream cheese,
  softened
16-oz. pkg. powdered sugar
1 T. vanilla extract

5 to 6 bananas, sliced
20-oz. can crushed pineapple,
  drained
12 oz. whipped topping
Garnish: pecans, cherries and
  chocolate syrup

Layer ingredients in the order listed in a 13"x9" baking dish. Decorate top of dessert with pecans, cherries and chocolate syrup. Refrigerate before serving. Makes 12 servings.

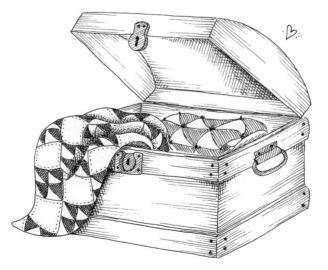

Comfort is...
A fluffy, goosedown comforter for your bed.

Apple Crisp

Marie Alana Gardner
North Tonawanda, NY

Each year in the fall, my mother and I go to the farmers' market, buy a bushel of apples and have an apple peeling party! We peel, chop, soak them in lemon juice and freeze them. That way whenever we feel like a nice apple crisp we pull some out and we're set to go!

1 qt. apples, peeled and cubed
1-1/4 c. brown sugar, packed
   and divided
1/4 c. water

2 t. cinnamon
1 c. all-purpose flour
1 t. salt
1/3 c. butter, melted

Place apples in a buttered 9"x9" baking dish. Add 3/4 cup brown sugar, water and cinnamon. In a mixing bowl, blend together flour, remaining brown sugar, salt and butter to make crumbs. Spread crumbs evenly over apples. Bake at 350 degrees for 50 minutes. Makes 6 to 8 servings.

Comfort is...
A child's first ride on the merry-go-round.

Fresh Blueberry Pie

Mary Baker
Fountain, NC

My best friend, Joni, brought this pie to a cookout at my house. It was so good that after everyone left, I had to pick some blueberries from my bush and bake up a pie...I just had to have one more big slice for myself!

8-oz. pkg. cream cheese,
   softened
3/4 lb. powdered sugar
16 oz. whipped topping

1 pt. blueberries
1 c. chopped pecans
2 9-inch graham cracker pie
   crusts

In a large mixing bowl, beat cream cheese until smooth. Gradually add powdered sugar; mixing and scraping the sides of the bowl until mixture is smooth. Add whipped topping and continue to mix until well blended. Stir in blueberries and pecans; mixing well. Pour mixture into pie crusts and chill before serving. Makes 16 servings.

Comfort is...
   Cute messages written in the steam on the
      bathroom mirror.

Cinnamon Bread Pudding

Justine Dillon
Charleston, IL

This is an absolutely fabulous dessert!

12 c. cinnamon bread, torn
1 c. raisins
1 t. cinnamon-sugar
6 eggs, beaten
6 c. milk
1 c. sugar

1 c. boiling water
4 T. margarine, melted
2 t. vanilla extract
1 c. sugar
2 T. cornstarch

Place bread into a greased 13"x9" baking pan; scatter raisins over bread and sprinkle cinnamon-sugar over all. In a separate bowl, combine eggs, milk and sugar; blend well. Pour over bread. Press bread down with a fork until bread is soaked. Bake at 350 degrees for one hour or until set. In a saucepan with boiling water, place margarine and vanilla. Mix sugar and cornstarch together and add to liquid mixture. Cook over low heat until semi-thick, stirring frequently. Pour sauce over bread pudding and serve warm. Makes 10 to 12 servings.

Comfort is...
Taking a road trip with your girlfriends.

Apple Harvest Tart

Nadine McKenzie
Ontario, Canada

*What a yummy dessert! It is so rich that we
save it for special events and holidays!*

1 c. all-purpose flour
1/2 c. butter
1 c. sugar, divided
2 t. vanilla extract, divided
8-oz. pkg. cream cheese,
   softened

1 egg
1/2 t. cinnamon
2 or 3 apples, peeled and sliced
Garnish: sliced almonds

Mix together flour, butter, 1/3 cup sugar and one teaspoon vanilla; spread on the bottom of a 9-1/2" round pie plate coated with non-stick vegetable spray. Bake at 350 degrees for 10 minutes. Blend cream cheese, egg, 1/3 cup sugar and remaining vanilla together and spread over the baked crust. In a plastic zipping bag, place remaining sugar, cinnamon and apples; shake until apple slices are well coated. Place apples on top of filling mixture. Sprinkle almonds over all. Bake at 325 degrees for 30 to 35 minutes. Makes 8 to 10 servings.

Comfort is...
*Coming around a bend in the road and
seeing the lights of home.*

Orange-Vanilla Cake

Molly Bishop
McClure, PA

This cake is fantastic on a hot summer day!

18-1/4 oz. pkg. orange cake mix
4-oz. pkg. orange gelatin mix
1 c. boiling water
3-1/2 oz. pkg. instant vanilla
    pudding mix

1 c. milk
1 t. vanilla extract
1 t. orange extract
8 oz. whipped topping

Bake cake according to package directions. While still warm, poke holes in cake with a fork. Mix gelatin with water and pour over cake; let cool. Mix pudding mix, milk, vanilla and orange extract together and spread over cake. Spread whipped topping over pudding layer; chill. Makes 10 to 12 servings.

Comfort is...
a card from your parents letting you know
how proud they are of you.

Chocolate-Mint Dessert

Carla Terpstra
Rockport, IL

*This is beautiful garnished with mint leaves
and crushed peppermint sticks.*

1-1/2 c. all-purpose flour
1-1/2 sticks margarine
2/3 c. chopped pecans
8-oz. pkg. cream cheese
1 c. powdered sugar
1 t. peppermint flavoring

green food coloring to taste
12 oz. whipped topping
2 3-1/2 oz. pkgs. instant
  chocolate pudding mix
3 c. milk

Combine flour, margarine and pecans; press into a greased 13"x9" pan.
Bake at 350 degrees for 30 minutes. Beat cream cheese, powdered
sugar, peppermint flavoring, food coloring and about 2/3 of the
whipped topping together. Spread over cooled crust. Combine
pudding with milk. Pour over cream cheese layer. Spread remainder
of whipped topping over all. Refrigerate before serving. Makes
12 servings.

Comfort is...
  Your first ice cream sundae of the summer season.

Strawberry Angel Food Dessert

Sheila Bailey
Watertown, WI

I like to serve this recipe at bridal and baby showers!

5 c. angel food cake, torn
3-1/2 oz. pkg. instant vanilla
   pudding mix
1 c. cold milk
1 pt. vanilla ice cream, softened

3-oz. pkg. strawberry gelatin
   mix
1-1/2 c. boiling water
10-oz. pkg. frozen strawberries

Place angel food cake into a 13"x9" baking dish. In a mixing bowl, combine pudding, milk and ice cream. Beat at low speed until blended. Pour over angel food cake; chill until firm. Dissolve gelatin in boiling water; add strawberries. Stir until cool. Pour over pudding mixture. Chill until set. Makes 12 to 14 servings.

Comfort is...
   Knitting baby booties for your best friend's twins.

Gooey Sweet Treats

Red Velvet Cake

Jane Bradbury
Circleville, OH

For a change from the usual birthday cake...try serving this!

1/2 c. shortening	1 t. salt
1-1/2 c. sugar	2 t. cocoa
2 eggs	1 c. buttermilk
1 t. vanilla extract	2 t. baking soda
2 t. red food coloring	1 t. cider vinegar
2 c. cake flour	

Cream shortening and sugar together. Add eggs, vanilla and food coloring. In a separate bowl, sift together flour, salt and cocoa. Add dry ingredients alternately with buttermilk; mix thoroughly. Add baking soda and vinegar. Pour into 2 greased and floured 9" pans. Bake at 325 degrees for 40 minutes. Cool and ice tops and sides of cakes. Place on top of each other and smooth icing. Makes 12 servings.

Icing:

1 c. milk	1 c. shortening
4 T. all-purpose flour	1 c. sugar
1/2 c. margarine	1 t. vanilla extract

In a saucepan, stir together milk and flour until thick and smooth over medium-low heat; let cool. Cream together margarine, shortening, sugar and vanilla; add to flour mixture.

Comfort is...
A couch, a quilt, a dog and a good book.

Sunny Banana Pie

Maryann Vincenti
Saddle Brook, NJ

The perfect summertime dessert!

1 banana, sliced
9-inch graham cracker pie crust
8-oz. pkg. cream cheese
2 c. milk, divided

3-1/2 oz. pkg. instant banana
   pudding mix
Garnish: shaved chocolate

Place sliced banana in pie crust. Mix cream cheese with one cup of milk until blended. Mix pudding and remaining milk. Pour over sliced bananas. Sprinkle chocolate over all. Cover and chill for 3 hours. Makes 6 to 8 servings.

Comfort is...
*Having the entire office remember
it's your birthday!*

Mom's Rhubarb Cake

Roxanne Bixby
West Franklin, NH

*A favorite summer dessert, made with freshly
cut rhubarb from the garden.*

2 c. all-purpose flour
1 t. baking soda
1 t. salt
1-1/2 c. brown sugar, packed
1/2 c. margarine
1 egg

1 c. milk
1 t. vanilla extract
2-1/2 c. rhubarb, cubed
1/2 c. sugar
1 t. cinnamon

Mix flour, baking soda and salt together; set aside. In a large bowl, cream brown sugar and margarine until fluffy. Beat egg into brown sugar mixture. Mix flour mixture alternately with milk into the brown sugar mixture until well blended. Stir in vanilla and rhubarb. Pour batter into a greased and floured 13"x9" baking pan. Combine sugar and cinnamon; sprinkle over all. Bake at 350 degrees for 40 minutes. Makes 12 to 14 servings.

Comfort is...
Learning to skip stones on a nearby lake.

Peanut Butter Pie

Dixie Barkley
Hope Hull, AL

Great for church dinners or to take to a friend who is under the weather!

3-oz. pkg. cream cheese
1/2 c. creamy peanut butter
1 c. powdered sugar

12 oz. whipped topping, divided
9-inch graham cracker pie crust

In a large mixing bowl, cream together cream cheese and peanut butter until well combined. In a separate bowl, mix powdered sugar and 1/2 of the whipped topping together; combine with cream cheese mixture and pour into crust. Frost pie with the remaining whipped topping. Refrigerate for several hours to set. Makes 8 servings.

Comfort is...
playing in the grass with your puppy!

Gooey Sweet Treats

Upside-Down German Chocolate Cake
Mindy Beard
Yorktown, IN

This is my dad's favorite! I make it for him every Father's Day.

18-1/4 oz. pkg. German
   chocolate cake mix
4-oz. pkg. flaked coconut
4-oz. pkg. chopped walnuts

8-oz. pkg. cream cheese
1 stick butter
2 c. powdered sugar

Prepare cake batter as directed on the package. Sprinkle coconut on the bottom of a greased and floured 13"x9" baking dish; sprinkle walnuts on top of coconut. Pour cake batter over coconut and walnuts. In a small bowl, combine cream cheese, butter and powdered sugar; blend to a smooth consistency. Take large spoonfuls of mixture and dot over cake mixture. Swirl together cake mix and cream cheese mixture. Bake as directed on cake box. Makes 15 to 18 servings.

Comfort is...
A jar of homemade strawberry jam.

Buttermilk Cake

Gwendolyn Runnels
Fairfield, CA

Moist and yummy...mmm!

1 c. shortening	1 c. buttermilk
2-1/2 c. sugar	1/2 t. baking soda
4 eggs	1 T. hot water
3 c. all-purpose flour	1 t. vanilla extract
1 t. salt	

In a large bowl, cream together shortening and sugar. Add eggs, one at a time, beating well after each. Add flour and salt alternately with the buttermilk; blend well. Dissolve baking soda in hot water; add baking soda mixture and vanilla to shortening mixture. Pour mixture into a greased tube pan. Bake at 350 degrees for 45 minutes. Reduce heat to 325 degrees and bake an additional 20 minutes. Makes 12 to 16 servings.

Comfort is...
Cutting daffodils from your garden
and sharing them with a friend.

Apple Cake

Sharon Coon
Edmond, OK

A favorite of ours...it usually tastes even better the second day!

3 c. all-purpose flour
2 c. sugar
1 t. salt
2 T. cinnamon
1 t. baking soda
3 apples, peeled, cored and diced

1 c. chopped pecans
1 t. vanilla extract
3/4 c. oil
3 eggs, beaten
Garnish: powdered sugar

Mix flour, sugar, salt, cinnamon and baking soda in a large bowl. In a separate bowl, mix apples with pecans and combine with flour mixture. In a small bowl, mix vanilla, oil and eggs together; add to flour mixture. Place in a lightly greased and sugared Bundt® pan. Bake at 350 degrees for one hour or until tested done. Let cool for 10 minutes and invert onto a serving plate. After cool, sprinkle with powdered sugar. Makes 10 to 20 servings.

Comfort is...
When your best friend knows exactly what's wrong
without you having to say a word.

Cream Puffs

Jane Granger
Manteno, IL

When I make this dessert, I have to make two because
my daughter has to take one home!

1 c. water
1 stick margarine
1 c. all-purpose flour
4 eggs
8-oz. pkg. cream cheese

2 3-1/2 oz. pkgs. instant vanilla
   pudding mix
4 c. milk
8 oz. whipped topping
chocolate syrup to taste

In a saucepan, bring water and margarine to a boil; remove from heat. Add flour and beat with a fork until it forms a ball. Place into mixing bowl; add eggs, one at a time, beating well after each. Pour and spread into a 15"x11" jelly roll pan. Bake at 400 degrees for 25 to 30 minutes; cool. Poke holes with a toothpick in pastry while baking to let the air out. Using a mixer, blend cream cheese; add pudding mix and milk; beat until smooth. Spread mixture evenly over pastry. When ready to serve, spread whipped topping over pudding layer and drizzle with chocolate syrup. Makes 10 to 12 servings.

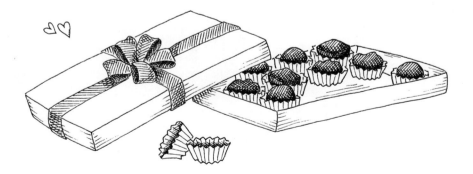

Comfort is...
a big box of chocolates!

Marbled Peanut Butter Fudge

Stephanie Moon
Green Bay, WI

Make sure you have plenty of frosty glasses
for milk...you'll need them!

3 T. butter
1-1/2 c. sugar
2/3 c. evaporated milk
1/4 t. salt
3/4 c. peanut butter

2 c. mini marshmallows
1 t. vanilla extract
1/4 c. semi-sweet chocolate
 chips

Bring butter, sugar, milk and salt to a boil over medium heat, stirring constantly. Boil for 5 minutes, stirring constantly. Remove from heat. Stir in peanut butter, marshmallows and vanilla. Stir vigorously for about one minute or until marshmallows are melted. Stir in chocolate chips until fudge appears marbled. Pour into a lightly greased 8"x8" pan; chill until firm. Makes approximately 2 pounds.

Comfort is...
A really good cup of coffee...with extra whipped cream and a dash of cinnamon.

Butterscotch Pie

Jan Sofranko
Malta, IL

Great served with coffee or cappuccino!

1 c. brown sugar, packed	3 egg yolks
5 T. all-purpose flour	3 T. butter
1/4 t. salt	1 t. vanilla extract
1 T. cornstarch	9-inch graham cracker pie crust
2 c. scalded milk, cooled	Garnish: whipped topping

Mix brown sugar, flour, salt and cornstarch together. Add milk gradually and cook in the top of double boiler until thick and smooth, stirring constantly. Cook for 15 minutes, stirring occasionally. In a mixing bowl, beat egg yolks until light and stir a little of the hot mixture into them. Add to mixture in double boiler and stir for 2 to 3 minutes. Add butter and vanilla; cool. Pour into pie crust and top with whipped topping. Makes 6 to 8 servings.

Comfort is...
Watching the kids spot Santa Claus at the holiday parade.

Gooey Sweet Treats

Velvety Cheesecake

Gail Hageman
Albion, ME

This is our traditional New Year's Day dessert!

1 c. graham cracker crumbs,
    crushed
3 T. sugar
3 T. margarine, melted
3 8-oz. pkgs. cream cheese,
    softened

3/4 c. sugar
2 T. all-purpose flour
2 t. vanilla extract
3 eggs
1 c. sour cream

Combine graham cracker crumbs, sugar and margarine. Press into the bottom of a 9" springform pan. Bake at 325 degrees for 10 minutes. Combine cream cheese, sugar, flour and vanilla in a mixer; beat until smooth. Add eggs and mix well. Blend in sour cream. Pour into a cooled crust. Bake at 325 degrees for 55 minutes. Cool before removing sides of pan; chill before serving. Makes 12 to 14 servings.

Comfort is...
Having the circus come to town...
and going to see it!

Chocolate Cabin Cake

Chris Beranek
Lamberton, MN

I first made this while on vacation with my family for my oldest daughter's birthday. Now, I make it for all 8 of my children's birthdays!

2 c. all-purpose flour
2 t. salt, divided
1 t. baking powder
1 t. baking soda
3/4 c. cocoa
2 c. sugar
1 c. oil

1 c. hot coffee
1-1/4 c. milk, divided
2 eggs
2 t. vanilla extract, divided
1 lb. powdered sugar
3/4 c. butter-flavored shortening
1 t. almond extract

Sift together flour, one teaspoon salt, baking powder, baking soda, cocoa and sugar. Add oil, coffee and one cup milk. Mix at medium speed for 2 minutes. Add eggs and one teaspoon vanilla; beat for 2 minutes. Pour into 2 greased and floured 9" cake pans. Bake at 325 degrees for 25 to 30 minutes. Cool at least 15 minutes before removing from pans. In a large mixing bowl, beat together powdered sugar, shortening, almond extract, remaining salt, milk and vanilla for 5 minutes; ice cake. Makes 10 to 12 servings.

Comfort is...
getting butterflies in your stomach every time you see that special someone.

Banana Pudding

Tammy Shaneyfelt
Hernando, MS

This is a perfect dish for family gatherings and church socials!

5-1/4 oz. pkg. instant vanilla
   pudding mix
3 c. milk
8 oz. whipped topping

16 oz. sour cream
3 bananas, sliced
30 vanilla wafer cookies

Pour pudding mix into a large bowl. Add milk; mix well with blender until pudding is creamy. Add whipped topping and sour cream. In the bowl you will be serving the pudding in, layer bottom with cookies, then layer with bananas, pour part of pudding mixture in; repeat layers and continue until bowl is full. Top pudding with wafer cookies. Makes 10 servings.

Comfort is...
Baby deer frolicking in a field together.

Index

Index

Desserts

Index

Index

Comfort is...
 Reading your favorite book over and over!

chocolate chip cookies • cheesy scalloped potatoes • rich chocolate cake • chicken & dumplings • caramel-apple pie • buttery mashed potatoes • warm homemade bread • cinnamon bread pudding • old fashioned macaroni & cheese • gooey chocolate

We've cooked up a whole collection of Gooseberry Patch® books!

Have a taste for more? Call us toll-free at

1-800-854-6673

We'll send you our latest catalog filled with snowmen, Santas, ornaments, candles, cookie cutters, gourmet goodies, salt-glazed pottery collectibles and MORE...including our best-selling cookbooks!

Phone us:
1·800·854·6673

Fax us:
1·740·363·7225

Visit our website:
gooseberrypatch.com

Send us your favorite recipe!

and the memory that makes it special for you!* If we select your recipe for a brand new **Gooseberry Patch** cookbook, your name will appear right along with it...and you'll receive a FREE copy of the book! Mail to:

Vickie & Jo Ann
Gooseberry Patch, Dept. BOOK
P.O. Box 190
Delaware, Ohio 43015

*Please include the number of servings and all other necessary information!

gooey CHOCOLate CHIP Cookies · CHeesy scalloped potatoes · RICH CHOCOLate Cake · CHICKEN & dumplings · Caramel-apple Pie · Buttery Mashed Potatoes · Warm Homemade bread · Cinnamon Bread Pudding · old-Fashioned Macaroni & cheese